Into the Fire: A Season of Navy Football, Fortitude and Faith

◆

John Owen

iUniverse, Inc.
New York Bloomington

Into the Fire: A Season of Navy Football, Fortitude and Faith

Copyright © 2008 by John Owen

All rights reserved. No part of this book may be used or reproduced by any means, graphic, electronic, or mechanical, including photocopying, recording, taping or by any information storage retrieval system without the written permission of the publisher except in the case of brief quotations embodied in critical articles and reviews.

iUniverse books may be ordered through booksellers or by contacting:

iUniverse
1663 Liberty Drive
Bloomington, IN 47403
www.iuniverse.com
1-800-Authors (1-800-288-4677)

Because of the dynamic nature of the Internet, any Web addresses or links contained in this book may have changed since publication and may no longer be valid. The views expressed in this work are solely those of the author and do not necessarily reflect the views of the publisher, and the publisher hereby disclaims any responsibility for them.

ISBN: 978-1-4401-0522-7 (pbk)
ISBN: 978-1-4401-0523-4 (ebk)

Printed in the United States of America

The opinions and viewpoints expressed herein are solely those of the author, and do not in any way represent the policies or opinions of the Department of Defense, Department of the Navy, United States Navy Chaplain Corps, or the United States Naval Academy.

Cover photo: AP/WIDE WORLD PHOTOS

Firefighter photo: John Labriola

All other photos: Phil Hoffmann

A portion of the proceeds from the sale of this book will be donated to the United States Naval Academy Foundation. www.usna.com

Learn more at www.john-owen.net

Dedication

To the 2007 Navy Football Team, and your teammates over the past 128 years.

You make us all proud

BEAT ARMY!

Table of Contents

Preseason: *Where's the Rule Book?* *1*

Week 1: Navy @ Temple University: *9*
    Into the Fire. [Daniel 3] *13*

Week 2: Navy @ Rutgers University: *19*
    We stand or we fall…together. [1 Cor 12:12-27] *23*

Week 3: Navy vs. Ball State University: *29*
    The man in the arena. [Genesis 32] *33*

Week 4: Navy vs. Duke University: *41*
    I choose to believe! [Joshua 24] *45*

Week 5: Navy vs. Air Force: *51*
    All in. [Deut. 6:1-6, Matthew 5:15-16] *55*

Week 6: Navy @ University of Pittsburgh: *59*
    Suffering, endurance, character, and hope. [Romans 5:2-5] *63*

Week 7: Navy vs. Wake Forest University: *69*
    Life without risk: the Big Lie. [Matthew 25:14-30] *73*

Week 8: Navy vs. University of Delaware: *79*
    You are writing your own story. [2 Samuel 11-12] *83*

Week 9: Navy @ Notre Dame: *89*
    A personal prayer. *93*

Week 10: Navy @ University of North Texas: *99*
    Remembering Goliath. [1 Samuel 17] *103*

Week 11: Navy vs. Northern Illinois University: *109*
    Learn, adapt, and overcome. [Jonah 2] *113*

Week 12: Navy vs. Army: *119*
    Be strong and courageous [Joshua 1-2] *123*

Postseason: Poinsettia Bowl, San Diego: Navy vs. University of Utah: .. 129
 Facing the Anakites. [Numbers 13-14:25] *135*
Epilogue: Spring Training 143

Preseason:
Where's the Rule Book?

♦

Head Coach Paul Johnson and an official discussing the finer points of a ruling.

PRESEASON:
Where's the Rule Book?

In the military, there is a manual for everything.

Except, apparently, for what it means to be the Naval Academy football team chaplain.

Consequently, while I was thrilled at being assigned to be the football chaplain for the 2007 season, I quickly realized that I had absolutely no idea what that meant! The only thing I knew for certain was that at each pre-game meal I'd be asked to give a brief devotion. Whatever that was.

As Navy's 2007 season unfolded, I began to develop a sense of how I, as "their" chaplain, could contribute to the team's efforts. Even more importantly, however, I came to more fully understand and appreciate what an amazing group of young men Navy football players are…and always have been. So while the 2007 season was an historic one in many ways for the Navy Midshipmen, it's the players and their commitment, determination and passion that left the deepest impression on me, and which I hope to share in these pages.

What is the role of a team chaplain? It's a question that occupied my thoughts throughout the season, and which I still ponder with fascination. Despite my non-existent "job description," I'd like to think that I got better at my job with every week. The team certainly did. Unlike the team, however, I didn't have a final score or game tapes to review to determine whether that was, in fact, the case. At one point, three or four games into the season, I made an appointment with Head Coach Paul Johnson to ask him whether or not he had any observations about how I was doing, and if he had any suggestions about how I might be more helpful to the team.

Now, I was forty-five years old at the time, with twenty-three years of military experience. I'd served as a helicopter pilot in the Coast Guard, a chaplain with the Marines, two Navy ships, and a Navy hospital. I'd been in some pretty stressful situations. But when I walked into Coach Johnson's office, I felt like a sixth grader interviewing the principal for the school newspaper. There is an atmosphere that surrounds big college football coaches that approaches reverence, and I was not immune to a bit of intimidation when I walked into his office. All that was missing was burning incense and organ music.

After chatting for a minute or two (I was well aware that the team chaplain was not number one on his list of concerns at the moment), I asked him if he had any observations or suggestions for how I was doing my job, and particularly if the devotions that I had given at the pre-game meal at the hotel every week were, in his view, effective and on the mark. He thought for just an instant, and then dead-panned, "well, they're different from the last chaplain." And that, it was clear, was all he had to say about that.

Coach Johnson, I observed, was a man of few words, and not exactly what you'd call a "warm fuzzy." He was, however, forthright and honest, and I was pretty sure that if I were totally blowing it, he would have told me. So in the absence of clear guidance to the contrary, I figured I was, more or less, on the right track. Which was of limited usefulness to know, since I still wasn't quite sure what it was I was supposed to be doing. So much for twenty-three years of military experience.

If Coach Johnson was reserved and non-committal in his feedback for the chaplain, Dr. Jeff Fair, the team trainer, was the opposite. "Doc" Fair, as he is referred to by, as far as I can tell, literally everybody, quickly became my most valued encourager, conversation partner, and mentor regarding the ways of Navy football. It was Doc who gave me what proved to be some of the most practical and valuable advice about how to be a good team chaplain. He was the one who suggested handing out some small token or memento from time to time (*"They love it when you give 'em stuff"*), and he's the one who encouraged me to come by the training room an hour or so before practice (*"They all have to come through there to get taped, and they don't have their game faces on yet, so it's easy to talk to them. Plus, you can learn who's hurt, and who might need a little extra encouragement"*). Doc has been a sports trainer since, I think, the first Roosevelt administration, and he knew every player, literally, inside and out. Rule One, then, for a football chaplain: get to know the team trainer.

The other obvious person to go to for guidance on my so-called "job description" was the previous football chaplain. At Navy, the chaplains rotate on a more or less yearly basis. A year is not exactly a length of time in which to build up a wealth of knowledge, but the previous year's chaplain offered one observation that proved to be absolutely critical. "When you talk to them before the games," he advised me, "don't expect a lot of feedback or interaction. They probably won't nod, they won't laugh at your jokes, they won't even change their facial expressions. They won't give you any indication they're even listening. But don't worry. They're just getting their game faces on. So just do your thing; they're listening to you. I think."

My predecessor's warning could not have been more accurate. Thanks to him, I was prepared with Rule Two for a football chaplain: don't expect a lot of feedback about how you're doing. If you need constant affirmation, this is probably not a good fit for you. Unless, of course, you do something wrong; then you'll hear about it from everybody.

Which leads me to Rule Three, which is actually not so much a rule, as it is a doctrine. Throughout our society, there is a lot of hand-wringing and gnashing of teeth about the appropriate role of religion in society. This is particularly true with regard to religion in schools. Not only is the Naval Academy a school, it's a *government* school, which introduces numerous additional layers of potential confusion and controversy about the appropriate place of religion. As a representative of religion working within a thoroughly secular context, it's important that I both understand and accept certain guidelines and restrictions on how I conduct myself and carry out my duties.

Official's Time Out

Whether it's appropriate for the Naval Academy to assign a chaplain to the football team, or to any other group of Midshipmen for that matter, is a legitimate question. Is having a chaplain speak to the team before each game consistent with the guidelines established by the Constitution? The reality is that there is widespread confusion and disagreement over how society, the government, and religion are to coexist and interact.

I am neither a lawyer nor a constitutional scholar, and I don't pretend to know all the answers. But I'd like to think that I've developed a practical, "common sense" approach to the issues involved which both respects the rights, and enhances the dignity and respect of everyone with whom I come into contact

Two primary considerations formed the basis of my approach to serving the team as chaplain, and, I believe, enabled me to positively contribute to the team's efforts without running afoul of some very contentious constitutional issues.

First of all, participation in anything I did was entirely voluntary, for myself and for the players, coaches and staff. I volunteered for the job, and nobody was ever compelled or pressured to talk to or listen to me. At every pregame talk I offered, attendance was voluntary, and in fact there were usually several people who chose to wait outside the dining room until I was finished. I took no offense at their decision, and in fact applauded it as a demonstration that they were willing and able to follow the dictates of their own consciences when it came to matters of faith and spirituality. On more than one occasion I approached players individually, because I had become aware that they did not consider themselves to be "religious," and I stressed to them that it was perfectly okay if they didn't want to listen to me. On every occasion in which I did this, the response was the same: "No, Chaps, I want to be there. I like listening to what you have to say."

There was no affirmation that I appreciated more than that. I was not there to force my religious views on anybody else. I was there to help the players become young men of character and integrity, on the field and off. Hearing them say that they found my words and my presence to be helpful and encouraging was all I needed to hear. And it convinced me that making opportunities for religious expression available to everybody, without making them mandatory for anybody, is both possible and beneficial for everybody.

The second consideration, then, in determining the appropriateness of making a chaplain available to the team ought to be whether it is beneficial to the Midshipmen, and supports the mission of the United States Naval Academy. The answer to these questions is, I believe, an emphatic, *yes!*

The pressures on all of the Midshipmen are immense. From reveille in the morning until taps at night, their days are filled with physical training, military obligations, academic classes, leadership development, Navy and Marine Corps history, doctrine and tactics, and a myriad of other requirements and expectations. It is quite an accomplishment simply to be accepted to the Naval Academy, or any of the service academies; it is an extraordinary achievement to remain there. The added stresses and expectations of a high-profile (and financially crucial) football program almost defy description. Any NCAA-level collegiate athlete works incredibly hard on the field. For Navy athletes, they are expected to compete at a national level *on* the field, and maintain the rigorous standards set for them *off* the field.

A chaplain can be a comforting, encouraging, and positive influence on these young men and women, just as chaplains serve those functions for active duty servicemen and women and their families in the Fleet. As football team chaplain, I was there to support and encourage the players, engage in conversations with them which they knew would not be shared with anybody else, and to help them develop into leaders of Sailors and Marines that our country can rely upon and be proud of. It was neither my job nor my desire to "convert" anybody, and it was never hard for me to reconcile my own Christian faith with my professional obligations and limitations. The team knew I represented the Christian tradition because I wore the cross as part of my uniform. But I was the chaplain for the entire team, which included anybody who came from a religious tradition other than Christianity, or no religious tradition at all. If I was doing my job, then what I had to say to the team every week was meaningful and relevant to *everybody*, regardless of what religious tradition they came from, or whether or not they came from any at all.

At the heart of everything I believe is the concept of treating other people the way I would like to be treated myself. There is, in my mind, no better witness to my own faith than this. Therefore, it was crucial for me to make every opportunity to speak to the team an opportunity to make what I was saying relevant for the religious and non-religious, the Christian and non-Christian alike. Was I successful in that task? That's not for me to judge. But the feedback I received from the players and coaches was overwhelmingly positive. And particularly gratifying to me was the fact that many of the most honest and meaningful conversations I had over the course of the season were with players who were ambivalent about religion at best.

The "ground rules," then, for a military chaplain—at the Naval Academy or on a Navy ship or with a platoon of Marines in the field—are built upon respecting the constitutional injunctions to allow everybody the opportunities to practice their religion freely, without compelling anybody to participate in any religious activity they don't want to. As the football team chaplain, these guidelines were always forefront in my thoughts and practice.

And so, armed with little more than a love for college football, a deep respect for what it means to be a Midshipman, and an intense conviction that I wanted to offer something meaningful to these guys while remaining well within the guidelines established for me by the Constitution and the Navy, I stepped in front of the team at the beginning of each pre-game meal. I shared my reflections with them on what it means to play football for Navy, and how their experiences on the field could help prepare them to be leaders of Sailors and Marines, and men of character and integrity. What follows in these pages are the thoughts I shared with the team from week to week, and some observations of how the things I was talking about in my devotions were reflected in the lives and efforts of the players as the season unfolded.

My season began on a miserably hot and humid July day (there is no other kind in Annapolis), when I stepped out onto the practice field for the first time, and tried to look like I knew what I was doing. It all came back to me…things I hadn't experienced since my senior year of high school: the smell of grass, the clacking of pads and grunts of contact, the hoarse bellowing and shrill whistles of coaches, the urgency, the sweat, the frustration. I was delirious, until a voice near me barked, "Hey! Who are you?"

I spun around, and found the apparent source of the threatening voice: a stocky, barrel-chested coach in Oakley sunglasses and a Navy ball cap. He was glaring at me. "Me?" I quaked. "I'm the new chaplain. I'm…".

"I don't care who you are! You're in the way. Move!"

It had been twenty-nine years since I had taken off shoulder pads for the last time. Playing college football was a dream I would never realize. In the intervening years I'd earned two academic degrees, had a family, flown over twenty-five hundred hours in military aircraft, and steamed across the Pacific to the other side of the world. Twice.

Standing there, it dawned on me…this was college football, and I was finally on the field.

Week One:
Navy @ Temple

◆

Senior defensive end Chris Kuhar-Pitters

One of the universal truisms of football, at any level, is that the inevitable nervousness that every player feels as game time approaches will rapidly dissipate as soon as the game starts, and you experience that first contact, the first hit.

As I paced around my Philadelphia hotel room waiting for the first pre-game dinner of the season, I knew the players were nervous. A 7:00 PM kickoff time means an entire day of waiting for the team, and there's nothing that excited, nervous and aggressive Navy football players like less than sitting around, waiting.

What I was entirely unprepared for, however, was how mind-numbingly, gut-twistingly nervous I felt. I worked on my devotion. I went for a run. I worked some more on my devotion. I took a walk around the hotel. I practiced my devotion. I took a shower. I looked at my watch. It wasn't even lunchtime yet.

Finally, the time came to get my uniform on. I had been advised repeatedly that whatever time the schedule said for an event, it would happen at least fifteen minutes before that. That was the way Coach Johnson did things. That was fine with me, because I was about ready to claw my heart out it was beating so hard. I headed downstairs fifteen minutes before Coach Johnson's fifteen minute early rule. He and the entire coaching staff were already there.

I don't know if every team is this way; I rather suspect it is. But as the players filed into the dining room, they looked as though they were headed for prison, not a nationally televised football season opener. There was no talking. Most of the players wore earphones and were lost in their own music. Nobody smiled, or even acknowledged anybody else. It was just as the previous chaplain had described it would be. The air was tense and electric. I tried to look cool and composed. If I looked anything like most of the players, particularly the Plebes (the first year players), I wasn't fooling anybody.

Coach Al Golden of Temple had issued the challenge early, never missing an opportunity to remind Temple players and fans how Navy had embarrassed them in the final game of the 2006 season by a score of 42-6. Former Temple and Navy coach Wayne Hardin had promised a crowd of sixty-six thousand for the 2007 opener, convincing the city and the school to host the game at Lincoln Financial Field, home of the Philadelphia Eagles.

Expectations were high for Navy as well, even though they had lost some key starters from the previous year. The defense, in particular, was going to have to prove itself. Paul Johnson was looking for his 100th win as a head coach. Navy had already been invited to the 2007 Poinsettia Bowl in San Diego, provided they finish the regular season with at least six wins. Navy was in the midst of one of the most successful stretches of football in its history, including four straight bowl appearances. The pressure was on to keep the success going.

One of the assistant coaches closed the dining room door. "That's everybody, Coach," he said quietly. Coach Johnson looked over at me, and gave an almost imperceptible nod. I stepped to the center of the room. I was sure my chest was about to explode. The players removed their headphones and stared at me.

My season was underway.

Into the Fire
Daniel 3

There is a story in the Hebrew Scriptures—what Christians refer to as the Old Testament—about three guys named Shadrach, Meshach and Abednego. (If any of you are fans of the "VeggieTales," you may remember these guys as Rack, Shack and Bennie.)

Anyway, here's the story. The king at the time, King Nebuchadnezzar, decided to have a statue of himself built. This wasn't a little statue, or even a life-size statue. This thing was ninety feet tall! And the King commanded that whenever the signal was given, everybody who heard the signal was to fall down and worship the statue immediately, or else they'd be put to death. Apparently the king had quite an ego.

Okay, fine. People were used to having to do what the King commanded, so no big deal. Whatever.

But Shadrach, Meshach and Abednego believed in the One God, the God of Abraham, Isaac and Jacob. And even though they had been employed by King Nebuchadnezzar, they couldn't, in good faith, bow down before his statue. And the king found out.

As you might imagine, the king wasn't happy that anybody, much less people who supposedly worked for him, would defy his commandments. And so he commanded that the three be brought to him personally. He said to them, "Look, you guys. I'm going to give you another chance. I'm going to give the signal, and as long as you do what you're supposed to do—as long as you bow down and worship my statue—you can go free. No problems. But if you don't, I'm going to have you thrown into a blazing fire, and no god will be able to help you then. So, c'mon, guys...what do you say?"

Well, Rack, Shack and Bennie told him not to even bother giving the signal, because they weren't going to worship the statue. They told the king that they were confident that their God would rescue them from the blazing furnace, and that they had no need to fear the king. And even if the king *did* throw them into the furnace, and even if their God *did not* rescue them, they *still* weren't going to worship the king's statue.

You can probably imagine how that went over. The king was done playing Mr. Nice Guy, and he ordered the fire to be stoked to seven times its normal heat. He ordered his strongest soldiers to tie up the three men and throw them into the fire. When his soldiers did this, the fire was so hot that when they threw Shadrach, Meshach and Abednego into the fire the soldiers were burned up!

Amazingly, however, the king saw the three men walking around in the furnace, apparently completely unharmed, and in fact they were talking with another person in the furnace! Stunned, the king himself called into the furnace and told Shadrach, Meshach and Abednego to come out, which they did. When the king saw this, and that they were in perfect condition—not a hair on their head was so much as singed—he acknowledged that the God of Shadrach, Meshach and Abednego was indeed very great, and he commanded that anybody, anywhere, who said anything bad about the three men or their God was to receive an even worse punishment than he had commanded for those who failed to obey his order to worship the statue of himself.

This is a very dramatic story, and of course it's satisfying because we who believe in the God of Abraham, Isaac and Jacob—the same God that Shadrach, Meshach and Abednego believed in—can feel a little smug about the fact that, in the end, God proved that he was greater than other gods, and the faith of Rack, Shack and Bennie was vindicated.

But there's a more subtle—and I think potentially more powerful—point in this story that's worth mentioning. Yeah, Shadrach, Meshach and Abednego had faith in their God, and they believed that if they did the right thing, and remained faithful, that God would save them. But they also made it clear that even if God did *not* save them, they would still not compromise their principles, or abandon their faith in God. Regardless of the outcome of this particular incident, their God was still the Lord God Almighty, and their God was the only god whom they would worship. They knew what they believed, and they trusted in their God, no matter what happened.

I have grown up watching and loving college football. Many of my favorite childhood memories involve going to UCLA games with my dad. He had played football there, and he taught me the twin joys of Saturday afternoon football, and rooting against USC.

Never, though, have I loved and enjoyed college football as much as I do here, at Navy. It's not because I'm an Academy alum...I'm not. Rather, it's because football here belongs in a much bigger and more important context. Not only do I get to watch you guys practice, but I also have the opportunity to observe and support you as you experience all of the "joys" of Academy life: Plebe Summer, formations, military training, class work, physical training. It is no exaggeration to point out that at most universities, football practice is the hardest part of the players' days. For you, that's not even close to being true! That doesn't mean that practice is easy—in fact, you practice as hard or harder than any team anywhere. But for you, the other twenty-one hours of the day are just as demanding as the three you spend on the practice field.

Even though all of you are working your hearts out to perform well on the football field, all of your work is in preparation for something you have volunteered to do *off* the field after you graduate. It's this bigger context that makes Navy football—that makes each one of you—something truly special.

The truth is that many of the teams we encounter this season will be better than you, statistically, anyways. But none of them—with the possible exception of the other service academies—can even come close to representing what you represent.

I want to illustrate what I'm talking about.

Look at the photo I've given each of you.

(COURTESY JOHN LABRIOLA)

I remember, six years ago, when I saw this photo for the first time. I've never stopped thinking about it. I don't know of a more powerful, inspirational photograph. Today, when I look at it, it reminds me of what I have chosen to do, and re-inspires me as to why I've chosen to do it.

In spite of its blurriness, you can tell exactly what it's a photo of. It's a New York City firefighter running up the stairs of the World Trade Center on September 11, 2001. And the most powerful, moving aspect of this photo is this: while everybody else is running *down* the stairs, away from the flames, the firefighter is running *up* the stairs, *into* the fire.

Gentlemen, that says everything. And that's exactly what each of you has volunteered to do. This is why we all are here, at the Naval Academy. This is why we wear the uniforms of our country. *We* are the ones whom our country is counting on to be willing to run *into* the fire, even as our families and loved ones and everybody else is seeking shelter and safety.

Is football of ultimate importance? Of course not. But it's here, on the football field, where you will learn crucial skills that will prepare you to respond when you are called upon to run into the fire. Here is where you will learn to steel your nerves and focus your wills when all the odds are stacked against you, and the obstacles facing you seem insurmountable.

Take another look at the photo. If you could look into his eyes, what would you see? Fear? Anxiety? Hopelessness? Determination? Maybe. Probably all of them, in various measures. Probably things that defy description. What matters, though, is not what's in his eyes, but the direction in which he's headed. Regardless of what his eyes see, or his mind says, or his heart feels, he's continuing up the stairs, into the fire.

Shadrach, Meshach and Abednego knew what they were up against. And they knew what they had to do. Regardless of how they might have felt, they knew their cause was right, and they remained steady in their focus. And regardless of whether or not God was going to save them, they were willing to step into the fire.

Virtually every time you step onto the field this year, there will be a hundred reasons why you should fail. There will be a hundred factors working against you in your efforts to win. A hundred naysayers every week proclaiming that you're not big enough, strong enough, fast enough, deep enough; you can't compete on a Division One level.

And yet every week, you'll steel your nerves, remind each other who you are and what you stand for, and you'll step out onto the field, and into the fire.

Because, gentlemen…that's what we do.

Game Wrap:

Many of the elements that would become common themes throughout Navy's season appeared in this first game against Temple.

Their triple-option offense started racking up the yards, and even though they stayed true to form by accumulating most of their yardage on the ground (361 yards rushing), they demonstrated the ability to strike through the air—including completions of thirty-seven and twenty yards—which further helped to provide room for their running attack. Junior quarterback Kaipo-Noa Kaheaku-Enhada led the offense to 439 yards of total offense, including rushing for 104 yards and one touchdown himself. (My eight year old daughter had broken my heart the previous week by announcing that she didn't like football. She prided herself, however, on her ability to pronounce Kaipo's entire name with all the ease of a native islander, every time she had the opportunity. Everybody else just called him Kaipo.) Junior slotback Shun White hit the ground running, rushing for 122 yards and a thirty-seven yard pass reception. Senior Adam Ballard came back from a broken leg he incurred against Army at the end of the 2006 season and scored two touchdowns.

On the defensive side of the ball, the picture was more mixed. Although they allowed Temple to complete twenty-one of twenty-nine passing attempts, Seniors Matt Wimsatt and Ketric Buffin each snagged an interception, and the defense held Temple to just seventy-four yards rushing.

Although Coach Johnson insisted that the team had a lot of improvements to make, it was, nevertheless, a good way to start the season.

Final Score: Navy 30 – Temple 19
Coach Paul Johnson got his 100th career college win as a head coach.

Week Two:
Navy @ Rutgers

✦

Junior fullback Eric Kettani

Another Friday night road game, which meant another day spent wandering around the hotel, working out, practicing my devotion, and checking my watch. And even though the nervousness was still there, it was different this week. It was less fear, and more excitement.

For one thing, I now had a sense of how things worked, and I could anticipate what the routine would be come game time. But even among the team, there was a different feeling.

We were in Piscataway, New Jersey, facing off against the fifteenth-ranked Rutgers Scarlett Knights, and the game was televised nationally on ESPN. It was an opportunity for Navy to play for the entire country, against a nationally-ranked team. Additionally, Rutgers was boasting an early-season Heisman Trophy candidate in running back Ray Rice, who was only sixteen yards short of establishing Rutgers' all-time rushing record.

More personal, however, for Navy was the fact that a year ago, Rutgers had humiliated the Midshipmen in Annapolis, 34-0. Early in that game, Navy starting quarterback Brian Hampton had suffered a season and career ending knee injury, and Navy never recovered in that game. This was a chance for Navy to avenge for the heavy price they had paid against Rutgers the previous season.

Navy takes some heat, from time to time, about the quality of the teams it plays, and the belief that it doesn't belong in the Football Bowl Subdivision (formerly Division 1A) of college football. This was a chance to reaffirm that in spite of the obstacles it faces when it comes to recruiting players, Navy was, indeed, capable of mixing it up with the big boys.

All in all, Navy had a lot to be excited about.

We Stand or We Fall...Together
1 Corinthians 12:12-27

Last week, I gave you a photo of a firefighter going up the stairs of the World Trade Center as everybody else was attempting to escape by running down, and I suggested that that image captured a really important aspect of who we are and what we do. As future Navy and Marine Corps officers, and as Navy football players, we cannot be afraid to head into the fire, because that's what we do.

I also shared a little bit about my own love for college football, and the fact that Navy football, and Navy football players embody, for me, the best of the sport. Being your chaplain is one of the biggest privileges, and biggest thrills, of my life.

But I have to also admit that I wrestle with what, exactly, my role is. And specifically, what's the purpose of these pre-game devotions? Part of me wants to give you a pre-game pep talk, get you pumped up for the game. But that's not my job. That's the job of the coaching staff.

I suppose I could approach this as kind of a mini-sermon, but church is the time and place for that, and this isn't church.

Some might suggest that it's my job to try to evangelize, or even convert some of you to the Christian faith. But there's a different time and place for that.

So what, exactly, is my job here? Well, to the best of my abilities, this is what I've come up with as my understanding of why I'm here, and what I hope to accomplish:

As you can tell from the cross I wear on my uniform, I am a Christian, and that is the faith tradition that I represent in my role as a pastor and chaplain. But one of the characteristics of Navy chaplains is that even though we each come from a specific faith tradition, and we are never required to do anything that contradicts our beliefs or ordination vows, we are, however, expected to help *all* of our Sailors and Marines and Coasties meet their spiritual and religious needs to the best of our abilities, regardless of what traditions they come from. What that means for me, here, is that, as the football team chaplain, I'm your chaplain regardless of what your faith tradition is. And I take that responsibility—and that privilege—very seriously.

My goal is to offer something to you every week that can help you integrate your beliefs with the way you live, on and off the football field. We should draw strength and inspiration from our faith, and I want to help you do that. I look at life through the lens of my Christian faith. If your faith is different, fine. My hope is that the truths and lessons that I glean from my Christian faith are applicable to *all* of us, regardless of what faith we come from. So my hope, every week, is to offer you some thoughts that allow you to find strength and inspiration that you can draw from on the football field, in your preparation as officers and leaders of Sailors and Marines, and in your development as young men of character and integrity.

Way back when the Christian church was just starting to form, there was a guy named Paul who understood his role to be a similar one. He believed his job was to help people understand what the teachings of Jesus of Nazareth meant for them in their real, everyday lives. He traveled a lot, and he wrote lots of letters to various new communities in the first century, encouraging them and helping teach them what it meant to be Christians. There was one church where the people were having a hard time getting along. There was lots of conflict and arguing, and so Paul wrote a letter to encourage and to clarify some things for them. In this letter, he used the analogy of the human body, and he pointed out that even though the body is made up of different parts, and each part looks and acts differently from the other parts, the body as a whole can't function properly unless all the parts are doing their unique thing and working with all the other parts doing their unique things. Some parts may get more attention and glory, but that doesn't make them any more important than the other parts. For example, the head gets lots of attention: it sees, hears, smells, talks, and we spend a lot of time trying to make it look good. The feet, on the other hand, get neglected lots of the time. We take them for granted, work them hard, and they often smell bad. But a body with a head but no feet has a serious handicap! And of course, feet aren't much good without a head to tell them what to do.

You get the point. The parts are all different, and unless they work together, the body as a whole can't function properly, and perform up to its potential.

Nobody understands this better than a football team. Certain positions may get lots of glory and attention, but they are only able to do well if the other positions do their jobs well. We may have the greatest group of running backs in history, but if there's nobody blocking for them, they can't do their thing. Every good football team clearly recognizes the importance of every position, and the importance of all the players working together as a team. You've all experienced those moments when there are no longer eleven guys on the field, but everything is working, you're hitting on all cylinders, and it feels like you're one body out there. That's one of the best, most exciting feelings there is, isn't it?

Okay, so every football team—every good team—has to understand this, to some extent. What makes us, Navy football, different? A couple things.

First of all, from day one of Plebe Summer, you've been taught that success is measured how…as individuals, or as a group? As a group! What matters is the *mission*, and individual success means nothing if the mission fails. So we're taught to think in terms of the *team*, and accomplishing the *mission*.

Additionally, we accept a willingness even to *sacrifice* ourselves for each other, and the accomplishment of the mission. You all, I assume, have seen or read, "Black Hawk Down." Do you remember what the soldiers said about what, in the heat of battle, they are fighting for… what keeps them going? The guy on their right, and the guy on their left. They are fighting to take care of each other, and their biggest fear is of letting their teammates down. Part of wearing the uniform means being willing to sacrifice ourselves for the good of our teammates, and the accomplishment of the mission.

And when we really "get it," we understand how much we need each other. Not only can you not do your job without my help, but I can't do mine without your help. *We need each other.* There's this great phrase in Paul's letter where he says that when the body, the team, is functioning at its full potential, each of the members holds the others in a position of honor, and nobody considers themselves more important than anybody else. "The members have the same care for one another. If one member suffers, all suffer together with it; if one member is honored, all rejoice together with it." That's the way Paul puts it.

Where is this truer than in football? Standout individual performances are great, but what really matters is the final score, right? How the *team* does. We succeed or we fail as a team. That's true on the football field, and it's true in the military. You may or may not be familiar yet with the concept of the MAGTF—the Marine Corps Air/Ground Task Force. It's the coming together of very different elements and capabilities—aircraft, artillery, armor, infantry—to form a single, integrated fighting force. And I'll tell you what, there is no more effective fighting force than a MAGTF, delivered and supported by the Navy. None of the individual components can do the job by itself, but when they come together and function as a team, nothing can stand in their way.

So here we are, playing on national TV, against a nationally ranked Rutgers team. And you know what? *All* of the pressure is on them! Think about it…only very recently has Rutgers earned national attention. They have an early season Heisman candidate. A career rushing record is on the line. Some high profile players are coming back from injuries. They are trying to prove they are a legitimate BCS contender. Everybody is watching *them*.

That works precisely to *our* advantage! They have all kinds of things on their minds; we have just one: working together as a team. Our success or failure is as a team.

Nobody understands teamwork better than we do. Absolutely nobody. Other athletes may understand it in terms of the game, but we understand that in a very literal sense our *lives*, and the lives of our fellow Sailors and Marines, depend on it. Nobody understands the importance of looking out for each other, nobody understands the concept of sacrifice, nobody understands working together to accomplish a mission better than we do. This is *our* undeniable edge every time we walk onto the field!

The Marines have borrowed an awesome image from one of history's great authors and storytellers, Rudyard Kipling. He wrote the original "*Jungle Book,*" among other classics, which includes these words:

> *Now this is the law of the jungle-- as old and as true as the sky;*
> *And the wolf that shall keep it may prosper, but the wolf that shall break it must die.*
> *Like the creeper that girdles the tree trunk, the law runneth forward and back:*
> *The strength of the pack is the wolf, and the strength of the wolf is the pack.*

An individual wolf, no matter how strong and fierce, can be brought down. But as long as the pack stays together, there's not much that they need to fear.

Each of you has different strengths, different abilities, different assignments. But you are a part of the same body, the same pack. We suffer, or we rejoice, as a team. Play as a team tonight. Swarm the field like a pack of wolves. We have nothing to fear.

Game Wrap:

The Midshipmen made Rutgers work for this one, but the Rutgers offense didn't miss many scoring opportunities. Several times, the Mids appeared to be fighting their way back, but crucially-timed mistakes and turnovers ultimately sabotaged Navy's efforts.

Once again, the loss against Rutgers was a costly one, as Navy unbelievably lost two of its most experienced and important defensive anchors to injuries: linebacker Clint Sovie and defensive team captain Jeff Deliz. Neither of them would return this season.

Final score: Navy 24 – Rutgers 41

Week Three:
Navy vs. Ball State

✦

Junior defensive end Michael Walsh

With two of its primary defensive starters sidelined indefinitely, the Navy defense found itself the focus of lots of unwelcome attention. What had been an inexperienced defense to begin with suddenly found itself patching holes with freshmen and sophomores. The sense of frustration was palpable, and the season was starting to look very uncertain.

Offensively, there was good news and bad news. Navy's running game was again putting up good numbers, already ranked sixth in the nation. Their passing game, however, ranked dead last. The key was going to be for Navy to control the ball for as much of each game as possible, and that meant making no mistakes, and no turnovers.

All in all, the pressure was really on. The Midshipmen were finally playing at home, and expectations were still high. Having inherited the most successful run in Navy football in decades, nobody wanted to be the team that broke that streak. For the team, however, there was the definite sense that the entire season could be on the brink of disaster.

For my part, I wanted to do everything I could do to encourage the team not to lose hope, not to get so caught up in the difficulties they faced that they let them become a self-fulfilling prophecy.

Class reunions are a regular occurrence at the Naval Academy, particularly during football season, and it's not unusual for there to be some pretty famous people showing up for their class reunions. As it so happened, the class of 1952 was having a reunion that weekend, and among the grads was a man I knew with whom my dad had flown in the Navy between the Korean and Vietnam wars. I showed up at the class banquet (uninvited, and very underdressed!) to say hi to him, and as I was about to leave, I had a thought. "Hey, isn't Jim Lovell in your class?" I asked. Yes, came the answer. "Is he here yet?" A few people looked around, but couldn't locate him. I hung around for a few minutes, but was starting to feel that I was overstaying my welcome, so I gave up.

As I was walking through the parking lot to my car, I saw someone walking toward me. Sure enough, it was Jim Lovell.

The poor guy never knew what hit him. Before he could say a word I had rushed up to him, shaken his hand, introduced myself, and asked him if he had any inspirational words I could share with the football team. To be honest, I'm surprised I heard a word he said, because inside my head were competing choruses of, "You're talking to a real American hero!", and, "You idiot! You're going to get yourself court martialed!"

Thankfully, Captain Lovell was more than gracious...although he did make a beeline for the banquet hall as soon as I let him out of my grasp

That was okay, though. I had what I wanted...

The Man in the Arena
Genesis 32

One of my favorite stories from the Bible is the story of a guy named Jacob. Jacob was the grandson of another guy named Abraham, who was the guy to whom God had come and made the promise that his family would be blessed by God in a way that no other family on earth had ever been, or ever would be. So Jacob was the third generation of this special family.

Up until now, the history of this family had unfolded in some strange and surprising ways, and Jacob was, in some ways, not a very ethical character. He had a twin brother, named Esau, who was a few minutes older than Jacob. In those days, that was huge, because the blessings of the father were passed to the oldest son, and their father, Isaac, was pretty wealthy and prestigious, so Esau stood to inherit a lot.

Jacob, however, was smarter than his brother, and was also his mother's favorite, and the two of them had come up with a plan to trick Isaac into giving Jacob the blessing that was rightfully Esau's. The plan worked, and Isaac unwittingly promised everything to his younger son Jacob, and once that promise was made, it could not be undone. As you can imagine, when Esau found out, he was furious. So furious, in fact, that he swore to kill his brother Jacob. And so Jacob fled the country to seek safety with his uncle in a different land.

Well, twenty years passed, and for a number of reasons Jacob—who had been very fruitful and successful—felt it was time to return home. Now, remember that his brother Esau had promised to kill Jacob, and in fact word had reached Jacob that Esau was on his way to meet him with over four hundred men. As far as Jacob knew, Esau had every intention of following through on the threat he had made twenty years earlier.

So it's the night before Jacob is to meet his brother Esau. He has sent everybody else in his family and community ahead in an effort to persuade Esau not to kill him. And in the middle of the night, when he's all by himself, he's attacked. And the story says simply that Jacob wrestled with his attacker all night.

Who was this attacker? Was it Esau? Was it one of his men? He didn't know, but he was in a fight for his life, and he fought with this unknown assailant all night long. Can you imagine how exhausting it must be to fight with somebody all night long? And then, at some point in the fight, Jacob's adversary strikes him in the hip socket so hard, that it dislocates his hip.

Now, I asked Doc what it would feel like to get hit so hard that it dislocates your hip, and Doc just kind of shook his head and said that he couldn't think of a lot of things that would be more painful. So picture this...Jacob's been fighting all night long, he doesn't know who he's fighting against, he can't beat this guy, but he won't quit either, and then this mysterious opponent strikes a crippling blow against him. I have to believe that at that point the adversary fully expected that Jacob would give up.

But he didn't.

In spite of his fear, his exhaustion, his excruciating pain, Jacob refused to let go, even though by now he must have known he couldn't win. Still, when the adversary told him to let go, Jacob refused to give up.

As it turns out, Jacob was wrestling God—or maybe an angel of God, it's not really clear—but either way, Jacob refused to let go until he received a blessing from this being. And the blessing that he received was a new name. "You shall no longer be called Jacob," the being tells him, "but you shall be called instead, Israel, for you have strived with God and with humans, and have prevailed." And this, incidentally, is the first time in the whole Bible that the name Israel appears. And what it means is, "Wrestles with God."

Incidentally, Jacob limped for the rest of his life because of that fight, but when he met up with his brother, Esau, all was forgiven, and Jacob—now called Israel—became the father of the twelve tribes of Israel.

Now, there are a lot of reasons why I like this story, and why I think it has a lot to teach us, regardless of whether or not we believe it's literally true.

Jacob had a lot to fear, and in fact he had prepared himself for the worst when he met his brother Esau, whom he had deceived. When Jacob was attacked, it was in the dark, and Jacob had no idea of the nature or the strength of his enemy. Once the fight was on, however, Jacob *refused to let go*. He simply refused to quit, refused to give up, in spite of his exhaustion and fear and pain. And finally, when all is said and done, it is this refusal to let go that earned Jacob—and all the generations of his family that came after him—a new name, and a new identity: Israel, "wrestles with God." And finally, even though Jacob was given a blessing that exceeded his wildest dreams, he was permanently injured, and was left limping for the rest of his life as a result—and a reminder—of this encounter with God.

Like Jacob, we have a lot to fear. Life has a way of sneaking up on us, and things happen that we don't expect, and sometimes we feel assaulted by circumstances and struggles that we can neither anticipate nor avoid. In the military, we don't get to choose all of our battles. Sometimes they are thrust upon us, and we are expected to engage with all of our strength and resources.

Even though we don't always get to choose our battles, however, we do always have one critical choice: how we respond. And even though there may be times when, no matter how hard we fight, we cannot win, we *always* have the choice to *not give up*. Victory will not always be ours to choose. But we can choose how we face defeat. Do we quit? Give up hope? Decide it's no use and stop fighting? Or do we hold on to the very end, play to the last whistle? Even when we are struck a crippling blow, we get to decide if we are done fighting, or if we aren't.

Now, in the military, it is often true that victory is the only acceptable outcome, and we train to fight for the victory, even at the cost of our own lives. But in most of life, defeat does not mean death. And in fact it is often the case that we are remembered not just by our wins and losses, but by how well we fought, how we carried ourselves, the virtues we demonstrated in the battle. Our battles often leave us with scars, seen or unseen; reminders of our struggles. We are not left unchanged by our encounters with life's hardships. But here, too, we decide whether we accept our injuries as reminders of defeat, or inspiration and experience for the next contest.

As you may know, the USNA Class of 1952 is having their fifty-five year reunion this weekend. And one of the members of the class of Fifty-Two is a guy you may have heard of. If you saw the movie, "Apollo 13," or, like me, are old enough to remember the real Apollo 13, you probably remember that they experienced an accident that very nearly resulted in the loss of the spacecraft and the death of the crew. And you may remember the name of the commander of that mission: Jim Lovell. Jim Lovell is a member of the class of Fifty-Two, and I decided that I wanted to meet him, so I staked out the parking lot of the banquet room where they were having dinner last night and I ambushed him as he walked in. Poor guy, didn't know what hit him, but suddenly there was this chaplain in his face introducing himself. He probably felt a little like Jacob, except that I didn't wrestle with him. But I did hit him with a question. "I'm the chaplain of the football team this year, sir, and you probably heard they experienced a couple of pretty critical injuries last week, and I was wondering if you had any words of encouragement, or advice about how to overcome adversity to offer to the team, based on your experience."

He was very gracious, and did not call the police on me, but he thought for a minute, and this is what he said:

There are two things that are critical when you face adversity. The first is leadership. And I'm not talking about the coaches here, the guys on the sidelines. I'm talking about the guys on the field, the guys in the struggle. People have to be willing to step up, wherever they are, and take charge, take responsibility for making things better, even if it wasn't their fault that things went bad in the first place.

And second, it takes determination. You have to keep going. You simply cannot give up. Even when it seems hopeless, even when it seems like the only thing to do is quit, you can't. Most football games are won or lost on the last yard, or in the last seconds. So many games are lost when guys simply give up too soon.

Whatever happens, you have to keep going.

And then he sprinted for the door and the safety of his classmates. But I had what I wanted. Words for you directly from the mouth of the commander of Apollo 13, Jim Lovell.

Leadership: not from the coaches, not from the people on the sidelines or in the boxes or the "experts" in the rear, but from the guys on the field. The guys in the fight. In other words, *you*. You have to be willing to step up and take responsibility for making things better, even if it's not your fault things went wrong, even if it's not your responsibility to make them better.

And determination: you simply have to decide not to quit. Even when you feel like there's no hope left for the outcome you were hoping for, you have to keep fighting. Once you give up, loss and defeat are a sure thing.

I know you've probably gone to great lengths to forget most of your memories from Plebe Summer, and most of what you had to memorize from "Reef Points," [the book of facts and information about Naval Academy life and history, large portions of which Plebes have to memorize during Plebe Summer.] But there is some really good stuff in there, and among the most valuable quotes, in my opinion, is the one from Teddy Roosevelt, commonly referred to as, "*The Man in the Arena.*" Do you remember it?

> *It is not the critic who counts, not the man who points out how the strong man stumbled, or where the doer of deeds could have done them better. The credit belongs to the man who is actually in the arena; whose face is marred by dust and sweat and blood; who strives valiantly; who errs and comes short again and again, because there is no effort without error and shortcoming; but who does actually strive to do the deed; who knows the great enthusiasms, the great devotions, and spends himself in a worthy cause; who, at best, knows in the end the triumph of high achievement; and who at the worst, if he fails, at least fails while daring greatly, so that his place shall never be with those cold and timid souls who know neither victory nor defeat.*

There is a lot we can learn from Roosevelt, and Jacob, and Jim Lovell.

Life is neither pretty nor easy. We don't get to choose our struggles, but we do have the opportunity to decide how we will confront them.

You don't get to choose your opponents from week to week, nor do you get to choose if or when people get hurt. Those things are not up to you. What is up to you, however, is how you're going to respond when you take the field. Are you going to make excuses, get discouraged, give up? Or are you going to step up and fill the gaps as best you can? Are you going to throw yourself into the contest with all the fury and determination and passion that you have?

The outcome of the contest is not necessarily entirely up to us, but how you conduct yourself on the field is. We will probably not be known as a great football team. But you can be remembered as a team that played every game to the last second, fought and scrapped every play for every inch of the field. You can be remembered as a team that refused to give up.

You will face adversity in your lives. You will face it on the football field, you will face it in your lives and careers, and you may face it on the battlefield. Football, of course, is not a matter of life and death. But how you deal with adversity on the football field can go a long way toward preparing you for when you encounter it on the battlefield.

You are the guys in the arena. Play to win, but whatever happens, *never* give up!

Game Wrap:

This game saw the continuation of some patterns that had emerged in the first game of the season against Temple, and introduced what would end up being a common element throughout the remainder of Navy's season: overtime.

Navy's offense continued to rack up the yards, and Navy's defense continued to give them up. The result was the first of several games that would come down to the final few seconds of regulation play or continue into overtime.

Once again, however, the game turned on two crucial Navy miscues: Ball State blocked a potentially game-winning field goal as regulation time ran out, and a Navy fumble set up Ball State's winning field goal in overtime.

Final score: Navy 31 – Ball State 34 [OT]

Week Four:
Navy vs. Duke

✦

Senior linebacker and team co-captain Irv Spencer

One-and-two was definitely not where Navy wanted to be four games into the season. It appeared to me that they were still a bit stunned from their loss to Ball State, and the defense, in particular, was struggling to find its footing.

The offense was, for the most part, starting to put up the numbers that the team hoped for, and would desperately need. Against Ball State, they accumulated an impressive 521 total yards, and again were firmly established as the top rushing offense in the country. Another hopeful sign was that Navy was also starting to put together a passing game, which would be an essential component in order to compensate for their defensive vulnerabilities.

As a result of the injury to Clint Sovie, the responsibilities of defensive team captain were passed to senior linebacker Irv Spencer. It would be up to him, along with the other co-captain, slotback Reggie Campbell, to lead the team through the season.

As it was early in the season, I was still getting to know the players, and I had not really gotten to know Irv yet. He appeared somewhat quiet, even hesitant, particularly compared to the volatile and fiery demeanor of Sovie. To be honest, I was a bit concerned about whether he was up to the challenge of that position, particularly in the context of the challenges that clearly lay ahead for the team.

At about five minutes prior to kickoff of each game, a referee calls for the team captains. On this day, the call came, and Irv and Reggie walked out the door and down the tunnel toward the field. I made it a point every week to position myself in a place where they would walk by me on their way to the tunnel, and I could give the two of them an extra word of encouragement. As they approached where I was standing, I called out, "Hey, guys…take charge out there!"

Irv looked at me, and I almost wanted to take a step backwards. There was an intensity in Irv's eyes that made it clear that I had not needed to say a thing. He was clearly ready to take charge. As he and Reggie walked past, I had the unmistakable feeling that these two guys were very, very special.

I was not wrong.

I choose to believe!
Joshua 24

The message today is actually very simple, but there aren't many realities of life and faith that are more universally true: the way our lives unfold is determined to a huge extent by the choices we make. There's no question that things happen in our lives that are completely out of our control, and that things happen that we neither expect nor ask for; even so, the choices we make in response to those situations can make all the difference in the way those incidents impact our lives.

Way, way back near the beginning of the story of ancient Israel, there were two leaders of the people who emphasized the importance of this very point. The first was Moses, the guy who had led the Israelites out of slavery in Egypt…a crucial turning point in their history. The people he was leading, however, in spite of how God kept bailing them out of trouble, kept making terrible choices, and as a result of their choices they ended up wandering around for forty years without being able to enter the land that God had promised them.

At one point, near the end of his life, Moses called all the people together, and he reviewed the history of everything that had taken place, reminding them of how God had always done what God had promised to do, even when the people had broken their end of the deal. As he concluded his speech, he presented them with this choice: you can choose life, or you can choose death. You can choose adversity, or you can choose prosperity. If you follow the commandments of God, you will make a choice for life and prosperity, and you will continue to enjoy and prosper from God's blessings.

If, however, you choose to go your own way, to ignore God's guidance and direction and decide that you know better, things will not work out well, and your choices will eventually lead to hardship and death. So I'm setting this choice before you: you can choose life or death, blessings or curses. Choose life, so that you and your children may live, loving the Lord your God, obeying him, and holding fast to him.

What Moses was saying is that God had promised to guide and bless them, but the choices that *they* made would determine whether or not they benefited from God's promises.

Not too much later, Moses died. His successor was a guy named Joshua. Shortly after taking on the role of leadership of the Israelites, Joshua, too, called the people together, and laid out a choice for them. In this case, they were on the verge of occupying the land that God had promised them. Joshua knew that it would not be easy, because it was a good land, and the people who were living there were not going to give it up without a fight. Like Moses, Joshua reminded the people of how God had been faithful to them, and then he presented them with a choice:

You can choose to trust God, Joshua said, or you can choose to trust other gods…either the gods your ancestors worshiped, or the gods of the people you are about to fight. But you have to choose. The people, Joshua knew, were at a crossroads, and they needed to decide now who they were going to serve, what they were going to believe. "So choose this day whom you will serve… As for me and my household, we will serve the Lord."

Two crucial points in Israel's history, two challenges to the people to make a decision about what they were going to believe. And the rest of the story unfolds as a result of the choices the people make, and the consequences of their choices.

Each of our lives is like that. There are crossroads, turning points, some big and obvious, others subtle and maybe even unnoticed, where we are presented with choices. And the unfolding of the rest of our lives depends on the choices we make.

I mentioned Jim Lovell, class of Fifty-Two, the commander of Apollo 13 last week. There's another guy from the class of Fifty-Two I want to tell you about. His name is Wendell Rivers, but everybody calls him Wendy. I first met him a few years ago at a reunion of the squadron he and my Dad flew in together. He is one of the gentlest, most humble men I have ever met. And he is, without a doubt, a true hero, although he'll vehemently disagree if you call him that.

Wendy was flying an A-4 Skyhawk over North Vietnam on September 10th, 1965, when he was shot down and captured. He was the thirteenth Navy POW taken during the war, and ended up spending seven and a half years as a POW, ultimately finding himself at the Hanoi Hilton with, among others, John McCain and Jim Stockdale. He told me a story about a certain night in his captivity, when he had pretty much reached the end of his rope. He had endured some horrific torture, had run out of hope, and was wondering if there was any reason to keep going. In a sense, he had reached a point where he was wondering if it wouldn't be better to choose death, rather than to continue with the hell that his life had become.

When things were at their absolute worst, Wendy says, at that moment, he looked up to the top of his cell, a six by eight foot concrete box, where there was one small window. Perfectly framed in that small window was the full moon. "At that moment," Wendy says simply, "I knew I was going to be okay."

Now, think about this for a minute. Did anything really change in Wendy's circumstances when he looked up and saw the moon? No. He was in exactly the same desperate situation he had been in the minute before. And yet at that moment something happened.

What happened was that, somehow, Wendy found the inspiration, the determination, to press on. For whatever reason, he made the decision to keep on fighting. He could have chosen differently. He could have given up. But he didn't; he chose life, and because of that decision, and many subsequent choices he made for himself and his life, he is around today to share his story. For Wendy and his fellow POW's, every day involved choices. He could choose to give up, or choose to fight a little longer. He did not have the power to change his situation, but he had the ability to look for little victories that allowed him to survive for one more day. Then one more. Until, for Wendy, seven years later, he and his fellow POW's found themselves on a plane going home.

"Today I set before you this choice: between life or death, blessings or curses. Choose life, so that you and your descendents may live."

There are two things we need to understand about the choices in our lives. The first is that even though we don't always get to choose our circumstances, or choose the way things happen in our lives, we *always* get to choose how we are going to respond. We may not always like the choices we have, but we can retain some measure of control over how our lives go by making the best choice we can in every given situation.

The second thing is this: there is a huge difference between *choosing* to do something, and *feeling* like doing something. Too many people make choices based on how they "feel." That is a one way ticket to failure. Feelings come and go on their own. They are random, unpredictable. And they are often wrong. I guarantee that there were days when Wendy and every other POW didn't "feel" like fighting.

Making a choice, on the other hand, is an act of the will. It is making a conscious decision to act a certain way, regardless of what we may or may not be feeling. Most of the important choices in our lives demand a deliberate determination on our part that we are going to act one way, or act another. The "right" choice often is different from the one we "feel" like making.

Think back on your football careers so far: how many days have you not "felt" like going to practice? How many times in a practice have you "felt" like slowing down, working at 70% instead of 100%? How many times have you "felt" like just saying, "forget it. I'm tired of this. I quit"? I suspect that you all have, at one time or another. But the important thing is that you didn't quit. Regardless of what you felt like doing, you chose differently; you chose to not give up. You chose to keep fighting; you chose not to quit.

Faith—in whatever you choose to believe in—is a choice; it is not a feeling. Believing in something is an act of your will, not a response to an emotion. We choose to believe, and then we act according to that choice. We choose to believe in God, or not. We choose to believe in another person's love, or not. We choose to believe in ourselves. We choose to believe in our team, our ability to keep fighting, to win. Or we choose not to.

Today I set before you the choice between life and death, blessing and curses. Choose life.

Choose this day whom you will serve; as for me and my house, we will serve the Lord.

None of us chose to be one-and-two at this point in our season. None of us chose to be playing without some key players. But here we are.

And now you have a choice. Keep fighting, or don't. Choose to believe in yourselves, or don't. It's up to you.

As for me, I choose to believe.

Game Wrap:

If it's possible to identify a turning point in the season, I think this game was it.

Every time Navy scored, Duke answered, and it very quickly became apparent that the outcome would be determined by who was the "last man standing." And, in the end, the Mids simply refused to give up.

Navy entered the fourth quarter down by three. Two of their primary point-makers were on the sidelines: Kaipo had played well, throwing for a career-high 217 yards, but had simply run out of gas. Starting kicker Matt Harmon had kicked a field goal and three extra points before suffering a groin injury. In spite of some impressive play on the offensive side of the ball, the defense had not been able to keep Duke out of the end zone.

Jarod Bryant—whose overtime fumble the previous week had resulted in Navy's loss to Ball State—entered the game for Kaipo, and sparked two consecutive scoring drives, including catching a touchdown pass from slotback Bobby Doyle that tied the score at 43 with 3:49 to play. Then the defense stepped in with a clutch play, as cornerback Ketric Buffin came up with his fourth interception of the season. The offense moved the ball down the field to the Duke twenty-six yard line, but was stopped twice for no gain by the Duke defense. With five seconds on the clock, Navy called time out.

Kicker Joey Bullen, although a senior, had lost his starting spot to junior Matt Harmon at the beginning of the season. Joey never got discouraged, however, and never quit working. He paced the sidelines as the clock wound down, and it became increasingly likely that it would come down to him. I grabbed him by the facemask at one point late in the game, looked at him and said, "Hey, you're ready." He looked at me right back, and said, "I know I am."

On fourth and eleven from the twenty-six, Joey trotted onto the field, lined up, and split the uprights as time ran out. The team exploded onto the field, and Joey was ecstatic.

I remember turning to Lieutenant Colonel Bob Benson, one of the officer representatives for the team, and saying, "If the rest of the season is going to be like this, I'm not sure my heart can take it." As it turned out, the rest of the season was, in fact, going to be a lot like that...

Final Score: Navy 46 – Duke 43

Week Five:

Navy vs. Air Force

✦

The Navy defense swarms the ball carrier.

There is no question that the rivalry between Army and Navy is as storied and legendary as any in all of sports. And it will always be the case that a large measure of success for any given sport in any given year at Navy will be whether or not they beat Army.

Less well known, perhaps, but no less intense, is the rivalry that has developed between Navy and Air Force, at least among the football teams. The perception at Navy is that Air Force is arrogant. The perception at Air Force seems to be that Navy is overrated. If you ask the Navy players, it boils down to this: Air Force does not respect Navy's football program.

Add it all together, and you've got the ingredients for a very intense and spirited competition. And this was never truer than this year. Throughout the 90's and early 2000's, Air Force dominated the match-up between the two teams; in fact they dominated among all three service academies. Navy had never beaten Air Force more than three years in a row, nor had a senior class at Air Force ever been denied the Commander-In-Chief's Trophy—awarded every year to the service academy team with the best record against the other academies—for their entire tenure at the Air Force Academy.

That all changed in 2006, when Navy beat Air Force for the fourth consecutive year, on their way to their fourth consecutive Commander-In-Chief's Trophy. None of this set well with Air Force, who considered losing to Navy "an embarrassment." Boasting a potential All-American and pro-candidate in wide receiver Chad Hall, and a nationally-recognized quarterback in Shaun Carney, Air Force promised to put Navy's besieged defense to the test.

The biggest advantage for Navy, perhaps, was that the game would be played in front of what would end up being an all-time record crowd at Navy-Marine Corps Stadium. In the end, that may have made the difference.

All In

Deuteronomy 6:1-6
Matthew 5:15-16

In the locker room after last week's game I said to many of you, "I saw your hearts today." All week long that's the thought that's been going through my head: I saw your hearts last week, and they are as big and as resilient as I thought they were.

And as that thought continued to reverberate through my head I thought of one of the sayings of Jesus that's recorded in the Christian Bible. Jesus was a great story teller. But he didn't tell stories to entertain people. Rather, he told stories because he knew that one of the most effective ways to get a point across or to teach people something is to teach it in the form of a story. He would often point to something very common and everyday—something people normally took for granted—and then he would use it to make a point. What makes this such an effective teaching tool is that from then on, whenever the people looked at that common, everyday thing, hopefully they'd remember the story that Jesus had told them about it, and they'd be reminded of what he had taught them.

So at one point, Jesus is talking to the people about living a good life, and encouraging the people to be different; to live as an example to others. And he points to a lamp—a common, clay oil-lamp, probably—the kind that everybody used for light, and he said, "Look. Nobody lights a lamp, and then puts it under a basket. That would defeat the whole purpose of lighting it in the first place. No, when you light a lamp, you put it on a lamp stand, and it gives light to the whole house. And so you need to let the light that is in you shine for everybody to see, as well."

Now the example he uses is simple and clear: nobody lights a light, and then hides it. What's the point of lighting a light in the first place if you're just going to cover it up? Everybody can understand that.

But then he hits them with his real point: each of you has some light, something to give to other people, something to teach them, some part of you that lights up a room or lights up a relationship. Don't keep that part of you hidden! A gift doesn't do anybody any good if it's kept locked up, if it isn't given away.

See, Jesus himself had grown up hearing stories. He was Jewish, and so he had grown up hearing the Scriptures read and the stories of his ancestors told and re-told. And one of the sayings from the Hebrew Scriptures that would have been the most familiar to him is this: "Hear, O Israel: The Lord is your God, the Lord alone. You shall love the Lord your God with all your heart, with all your soul, and with all your might." This phrase is sometimes referred to as the "Shema," which is Hebrew for, "Hear." In a sense it might be considered Judaism's "Great Commandment." It forms the foundation for everything Jesus learned, believed, and taught.

Here's the reason I mention this: notice the wording…notice that it doesn't tell us to love God with part of ourselves, love others with another part, love our jobs with another part. No, what it says is we are to love God with *all* our heart, with *all* our soul, and with *all* our might. There is no room for half measures here, no conditional commitments, no partial promises. No, the heart and soul of the Jewish and Christian faiths is that we are to commit ourselves *completely* to our relationship with God. We are called to be *all in*.

That's a phrase that's familiar to us: *all in*. It defines everything we're about at Navy. And while Jesus and his Jewish faith understood that concept to form the foundation of their religion, we understand that concept to form the foundation of everything we're about as a football team. And it also, by the way, is a pretty good reflection of what we are called to commit in our service to our country.

All in. No half measures. Bring what you have, and lay it all out there.

Here's the catch: when you go all out, you're going to make some mistakes. That's not a "maybe," it's a definitely. But if you let a fear of making mistakes hold you back from throwing yourself heart, soul and strength into a task, the result will be a devastating mediocrity. Being "just good enough" is not what we're about.

Now you know that you're going to have to bring everything you have to the field today. You know that Air Force certainly will. They've got a chip the size of Texas on their shoulders. But more importantly, I want you to understand just how important this concept is in your development as leaders of men and women, of Sailors and Marines. You have got to be willing to throw yourself heart, mind, body and soul into a task, and to inspire your shipmates and fellow Marines to do the same. You have to let your abilities shine for everybody to see, so that they can learn, and be inspired and motivated to let their light shine, and commit themselves to the cause. When you go all in, it inspires those around you to go all in, as well.

I saw your hearts last week. Everybody did. And they were spectacular. Magnificent. Now don't put them back under a basket. Don't hide them away for some undefined future. Bring them to everything you do, on and off the field. Let them shine. Throw yourselves into the challenges you face with all your heart, with all your soul, and with all your strength. Don't hold back. Be *all in*.

Game Wrap:

This was a day on which the Navy players were, indeed, all in, and a combination of terrific individual performances and effective team play allowed the Midshipmen to play an even more inspired game than they had a week earlier.

While the two teams traded scores for much of the game, Navy managed to break a couple of big plays—including a breath-taking seventy-eight yard touchdown run by quarterback Kaipo-Noa Kaheaku-Enhada in the fourth quarter—that proved to be the difference.

Additionally, the defense did their best to silence the critics. Even though Air Force racked up a lot of yardage, the defense held fast when it counted, preventing Falcon scores four times from inside the red zone, including a fourth and one from the Navy five yard line. In my opinion, this exemplifies one of the most inspirational aspects of the entire season.

All season long, the defense was consistently questioned and criticized. While much of the criticism was justified, it nonetheless had to be very frustrating and demoralizing for the players. And yet they never quit, and in fact, time and again throughout the season they came through in the clutch. At this point in the season, Navy had started about twenty different players on defense, both as a result of injuries, and as Defensive Coordinator Buddy Green and his staff worked to find the best combination of experience and ability. Younger players were expected to step up very quickly, and much more was expected of the more experienced players.

What the defense lacked in experience and ability, they made up for in attitude and in heart. In this respect, I think the Navy defense ended up being one of the success stories of this season.

Final Score: Navy 31 – Air Force 20

Week Six:
Navy @ University of Pittsburgh

✦

Senior placekicker Joey Bullen

Under dark, threatening skies we boarded the buses for the ride to Heinz Field in Pittsburgh, our first road game in a month. Once again, it had been a long day of waiting, as kickoff wasn't scheduled until 8:00 PM, and once again, we were playing in front of a national television audience.

The season had taken on a distinctly different feeling with the win over Air Force, and the resulting three-and-two record. There was a new sense of hope, and a definite boost in confidence throughout the team. That's not to say that there was any noticeable change in the team's pre-game routine—the mood was as serious and somber as ever, perhaps even more so. But I had a feeling that the team was starting to believe in themselves with a renewed sense of conviction.

"A blank canvas." That's what Coach Johnson called the game ahead when he spoke briefly to the team before leaving the hotel. And that's exactly what it felt like: exciting, full of possibilities, and yet excruciatingly uncertain at the same time. The bottom line, Coach Johnson stressed, was that it was up to the team to decide how the canvas looked at the end of the game.

For me personally, this game provided a kind of "crisis" point; not in the sense of looming disaster, but as a moment in which several streams of thought and reflection converged as I considered my role as team chaplain, and the questions the job raised for me:

- *What is the role and purpose of a "team chaplain"? To encourage and motivate the players? Or is there more to it than that? And what about the coaches...what is my responsibility to them?*

- *What do I pray for...as a chaplain? ...as a fan? I can't deny sending up prayers of, "Please, God, we need a touchdown," with a fervency equal to many of my prayers for guidance or healing! Is that bad? Do I need to ask forgiveness for those prayers? [I can only hope that God has a good sense of humor. Or that God is a college football fan.] Obviously I prayed for safety and courage for all the players. But what else should I be praying for?*

- *How do you motivate people? How do I convey relevant ideas to these young men with honesty, conviction and the genuine love that I feel for them?*

- *Why does football seem so important, and elicit such passion? And how can I take advantage of that passion and help the players direct it toward their preparation as officers of Sailors and Marines, leaders of young men and women?*
- *If faith is real, then it must be relevant to every facet of our lives. How can I model genuine and relevant faithfulness, staying true to my beliefs, while respecting constitutional boundaries and the beliefs and decisions of others?*

For whatever reason, all of those questions seemed to cascade around me as we drove to the game against the Pitt Panthers.

Walking to the locker room of the stadium where the legendary Pittsburgh Steelers play, Lou Holtz walked past. I looked over my head, where huge pipes ran along the corridor overheads, labeled, "hot water," "cold water," "steam," and, "beer."

Welcome to Pittsburgh.

Suffering, endurance, character, and hope.
Romans 5:2-5

In the Navy and Marine Corps, we have a set of Core Values. You know what they are: honor, courage, commitment. These are the values, the personal characteristics that are at the heart of what we aspire to be as Sailors and Marines.

It seems to me that we might also identify a set of core values for football players, and for spiritual people, whatever form one's spirituality might take.

If the coaches were to get together to define a set of core values for us as a team, I suspect it would look very similar to this: toughness, selflessness, and attitude. We talk a lot about all of them, particularly the last one. Our t-shirts even say it: "Talent is something; Attitude is *everything."*

As spiritual or religious people, regardless of what religious tradition we come from, a set of core values might look something like this: faith, hope, and love. I think it's safe to say that those are core characteristics of virtually any religious or spiritual tradition.

Now, identifying a set of so-called "core values" might be a nice gesture, and it might make for a catchy phrase, but they aren't worth much if they don't serve a purpose...if they don't offer us something to help us in our real lives. And as I looked at these three sets of core values, it struck me that one of the things that they have in common is that they all spring from a fundamental assumption about life. And that starting point is this: we will encounter adversity in our lives. Something will stand in the way between us and the accomplishment of our goals. And these core values stand as reminders of what it will take to successfully face the adversity, and opposition, and even suffering that will inevitably come into all our lives.

Ironically, our culture hates this fundamental assumption. It hates it so much that it tries to pretend it isn't true. Our culture tries desperately to insist that it is, in fact, possible to be happy all the time, to have everything you want, to accomplish anything. And in fact our culture even goes so far as to suggest that if you *aren't* getting everything you want in life, you're doing something wrong. You're not working hard enough, you're not taking the right drugs, you're not doing the right job, you don't know the right people. Adversity is the enemy. Pain is to be avoided at all costs.

Even many religious people fall into this trap, insisting that if you're suffering, you must have done something wrong; you must have done something to earn God's displeasure. Wealth and success are seen as signs that God has blessed you. The problem with this way of thinking is that it simply ignores not only the holy scriptures of virtually every religious tradition I'm aware of, but it utterly overlooks the overwhelming evidence of several thousand years of human existence.

And yet our culture persists in thinking this way, and where it really impacts us is in this: there are a lot of people out there who simply cannot understand why anybody would join the military, and willingly put themselves at risk. Why would anybody in their right mind volunteer to undergo hardship?

Now, don't get me wrong. There have been plenty of days in my military career when I've asked myself, "what was I thinking when I signed up for this? This is ridiculous!" No doubt you have had those days as Midshipmen. You've probably had them as football players, too. Days when you wondered why the heck you were voluntarily submitting yourselves to inhuman workouts in ungodly heat, willingly surrendering hours of precious sleep in order to sweat and hurt and get yelled at.

And yet, we continue to submit ourselves to hardship and pain. We have, in fact, volunteered to accept adversity, pain, and even danger as part of what we do. Why? Because we see our efforts as part of a larger purpose. And we believe that it's a purpose that is worth suffering for. *We understand that some things are worth pursuing, even at the cost of pain and suffering, even in the face of fierce resistance.*

In spiritual terms, the core value that defines and addresses this characteristic of ours that allows us to see beyond our immediate circumstances to the larger purpose that lies behind our efforts, is hope. Of the three spiritual core values that I mentioned, faith, hope, and love, hope perhaps gets the least attention. And yet it is at least as important and valuable as the other two.

Hope is what tells us to *never* give up. It's what compels us to keep fighting. It's what pushes us forward, even when every bone in our body wants to sit down and quit.

Let me tell you what hope is not: hope is *not* wishful thinking. Hope is not sitting still and waiting for the situation to change. True hope is not passive; it is aggressive. It inspires action; it fuels the will. Hope drives us forward, even at the cost of pain and suffering. Even in the face of fierce resistance.

There's a great phrase from the Christian Bible that absolutely nails this concept. It encourages us not to be afraid of suffering, because, "…suffering produces endurance, and endurance produces character, character produces hope, and hope does not disappoint us…" If you ever feel like the Bible is out of touch with the reality of your life, read that statement again, because it is perfectly on target! Think about how it applies to you as football players: you willingly suffer through practice, because with practice your endurance improves. As your endurance improves, you realize that you can do more than you thought you can do; it builds your character. And when you develop character, you recognize that some goals are worth pursuing even at a cost, and so you look past the short term pain, to the long term goal. And that is called hope. And once you have hope, you can never really be beaten, because true defeat only happens when we accept it. As long as we have hope, we are never beaten.

Think back to Wendy Rivers and Jim Lovell, among others. There are any number of times when it would have been understandable for them to give up. They were beaten; their goals had slipped from reach. And yet they refused to give up…what? Hope. And because they did not give up their hope, their hope did not let them down. And this is crucial: hope **cannot** be taken from us. It can only be given up. When the adversary breaks our will, compels us to give up our hope, then we are truly beaten.

On the contrary, as long as we hold on to hope, we are never truly beaten.

So, then: Suffering helps build our endurance; endurance builds character. Character is that part of us that has been tried and tested, and knows that it can survive. There is a confidence that comes with character, a resilience that compels us to, as a former Commanding Officer of mine used to exhort the crew, "keep your heads up and your chests puffed out." As our character grows, so does our hope. And as long as we have hope, we can never be truly beaten.

Here, again, is why football is so relevant to your preparation to lead Sailors and Marines. We know there will be opposition. We expect it, we plan for it, we learn to resist and endure it. It would not be football if there wasn't an opposing team. And we know that the opposing team is going to want to win as badly as we do, and they will do everything in their power to stop us from accomplishing our goals.

Knowing this, do we shrink from the game? Absolutely not! We prepare for it, and we thrill in it.

In the same way, you well know that there are people out there who, at this moment, are preparing to oppose you, even to kill you. I don't know the circumstances—when or where it will happen—but I guarantee you that at some point you will encounter a situation in which some combination of factors will be conspiring to cause you to fail, to give up hope, to give up without accomplishing your mission. But I also know that how you respond to that situation will depend largely on how you learn to deal with opposition on the football field. At some point you will find yourself reaching back into your heart and experience and finding some measure of courage, of determination, of hope, that you learned on the football field, and it will serve you well.

Suffering and adversity develop endurance. Endurance produces character. Character leads to hope, and hope does not disappoint us.

As long as you have hope, you can *never* be truly beaten.

Game Wrap:

Standing on the sidelines during the pre-game warm-ups, an elderly, distinguished gentleman walked up to me. He asked who I was, held out his hand and said, "Hi, Chaplain, good to meet you. My name's John Majors."

I'm pretty sure I made a complete idiot out of myself. "Johnny Majors? Coach Johnny Majors? Wow, what a pleasure to meet you, sir!" The legendary, national championship-winning coach was very patient with me. He waited until I stopped tripping all over myself, smiled, and said, "I was wondering if you'd tell Coach Johnson I came by. He's a terrific coach and I have great respect for him."

"Of course, I'd be happy to tell him. What a privilege to meet you... Coach!" He smiled, and continued down the sideline. I stood there, bewildered, looking around and babbling to nobody in particular, "Johnny Majors! That was Johnny Majors!"

A few minutes later, Heisman Trophy-winners and subsequent Dallas Cowboys teammates Roger Staubach (Navy) and Tony Dorsett (Pitt) appeared together at midfield.

I should have known it was going to be a special night.

It's a good thing I come from a family that has strong hearts, because otherwise mine would have given out by the end of the game. In a back and forth contest, where the two teams seemed to trade score for score, it shaped up to be another game of, "last man standing."

With regulation time running out, Joey Bullen attempted a winning forty-eight yard field goal but came up short. The first overtime lasted all of seven plays, with Pitt taking advantage of a Navy penalty to score a touchdown, and Kaipo finding Reggie Campbell in the end zone on the very next play to tie the score and bring on the second overtime.

Joey's field goal from twenty-nine yards out put Navy ahead. On fourth and goal from the two, Pitt went for the win rather than the tie. Navy cornerback Rashawn King was all over Pitt receiver Darrell Strong as he dove for a pass in the corner of the end zone. The ball and both players sailed out of bounds, and the game was over. It was Navy's first-ever overtime win.

I wrote in my journal that night, "The elation of a win like this is hard to describe. It's pure joy—absolute fun. In the end, it's fleeting. But it sure is fun while it lasts...".

And that, friends and neighbors, is college football.

Final Score: Navy 48 – Pitt 45 (2 OT)

Week Seven:
Navy vs. Wake Forest

✦

Junior quarterback Kaipo-Noa Kaheaku-Enhada

It may have been Navy's Homecoming, but defending ACC champion Wake Forest was coming to Annapolis with a full head of steam, having just recorded a huge win over Florida State. It had been a year earlier, in their 2006 Homecoming game, that Navy had suffered a devastating 34-0 loss to Rutgers, and the even greater loss of starting quarterback Brian Hampton.

Stepping in for Hampton that day was a Youngster (Sophomore) quarterback named Kaipo-Noa Kaheaku-Enhada. He had held the starting QB position ever since.

Kaipo had clearly established himself as the spark behind the Navy triple-option offense. He had rushed for over one hundred yards in four of Navy's six games so far in the season, and was the team leader in rushing yards (536) and rushing touchdowns (eight). Additionally, his improvement as a passer was remarkable, having thrown for 626 yards and four touchdowns. By comparison, Navy had thrown for 728 yards in the entire 2006 season!

On the one hand a typically laid-back Hawaiian, he was also an intense competitor; nobody was harder on him than he was on himself when he did not feel that he rose to meet the level of performance that was expected of him. At the same time, he seemed to thrive on pressure. I know I'm jumping ahead here, but a perfect example of Kaipo's competitive spirit occurred two weeks later against Notre Dame. It was late in the game, and Navy had the ball on an important third or fourth down play. Time out had been called, and Kaipo had the offense lined up on the ball, ready for the refs to resume play. The Notre Dame crowd was deafening, and yet Kaipo danced around the backfield, bobbing his head, waving his arms and encouraging the Irish crowd to get louder. His smile was so big you could see it from the sidelines. For Kaipo, this was not grandstanding, nor was it taunting. He simply could not wait to get back to the game. One of the Notre Dame defensive linemen waved his arms as well, mimicking Kaipo. Kaipo responded by bouncing up to the line, still grinning, and swapping a high five with the lineman. It was a pure Kaipo moment. Since taking the helm of Navy's offense a year earlier, Kaipo had demonstrated increasing comfort and competence in his leadership role on and off the field.

The beleaguered Navy defense had taken another hit against Pitt the previous week, with the loss of Junior defensive back Ketric Buffin. "Buff's" loss was significant, in that he had snagged four interceptions thus far in the year…one of Navy's few defensive bright spots.

Everybody knew this was going to be a very tough game.

Life without risk...the Big Lie
Matthew 25: 14-30

As I'm sure you all know, what fundamentally defines Christians is their belief that Jesus was the Son of God, in a way that no other human being before or since will ever be. What you may not know, though, is that many other religious traditions also recognize Jesus as somebody special...a prophet, a unique and powerful teacher. And one of the things that made Jesus such an effective teacher was the way he used stories to make a point, and to teach very important concepts. We call many of these stories, "parables."

In one of his stories, Jesus tells about a man who was going away on a trip, and decided to entrust his estate and his wealth to three of his servants. Now, the Bible uses the term "talent" to describe the amounts of money that he distributed to each servant. Historians tell us that a "talent" was an amount of money equivalent to fifteen years' wages for a common laborer. The point is that a "talent" was a relatively large amount of money.

So in this story, the man calls his first servant, and gives him five talents. Then he calls his second servant and gives him two, and then gives one talent to his third servant. They he goes away.

The first servant takes this chunk of his master's money and he trades with it, and he makes five more talents. The second servant, the one with two talents, does the same thing, and has similar results:

he makes two additional talents. The third servant, however, takes his master's money, digs a hole in the ground, and buries it.

After a long while, the master comes back, and of course he wants an accounting of his money. So one at a time he calls his three servants back to settle up. The first servant comes to him and says, "Master, you gave me five talents. I took them, and traded with them, and made five more talents." The master is very pleased with this result, and you can understand why. This servant had doubled his money! "Well done, good and faithful servant," the master says. "Because you have been trustworthy in this task, I will give you greater, more important tasks to do. Enter into the joy of your master."

Now, to be honest, I'm not exactly sure what he meant by, "enter into the joy of your master," but the point is that the master is obviously very pleased with the trustworthiness and performance of this first servant.

The second servant comes to the master, and he likewise says, "Master, you gave me two talents. I took them, and traded with them, and made two more talents." And once again, the Master is thrilled. "Well done, good and faithful servant," the master says. "Because you have been trustworthy in this task, I will give you greater, more important tasks to do. Enter into the joy of your master."

Then the third servant arrives, and says to his master, "Sir, I knew that you were a harsh man, and that you make your living off of the work of others, and I was afraid of what you might do to me if I lost your money, so I buried it for safekeeping. Here it is, exactly what you gave me."

The master goes ballistic. "You wicked and lazy slave," he yells. "If you knew me to be harsh, and if you knew that I expected other people to make me more money, then you should have at least put the money in the bank where it would have earned interest. So, since I can't even trust you to do that, I'm taking everything away from you and giving it to my other servants. Because here's how it works: to the people who know how to use what they have, even more will be given. But for those who squander what little they have, they will end up with nothing. As for you, you worthless slave, I'm going to have my boys take care of you and throw you out with the trash, where you belong."

Now, that's not exactly the wording that the Bible uses, but I think that's basically the point. The master is furious with this servant for not even trying to do anything productive with what he'd been given, and he kicks him out and tells him never to come back.

So that's the story; let me point out a couple of specific things about it. First of all, the master did not give the servants the same amount. Apparently, he saw differing abilities in each of them, and so he gave them varying amounts of responsibility. Secondly, these were not inconsequential sums of money he was handing out! If one talent equals fifteen years' wages, then five or two or even one talent is a pretty good amount of money. And finally, when he comes back, and sees the results of his first two servants, he is equally pleased with both. They both get the same response from him, even though the amounts of money they made for him were not equal. With the third servant, however, what appears to make him so mad is that the third servant didn't even try to do *anything* with it! He just buried it, and gave it back to his master exactly as it had been given to him.

When I hear this story, I can't help but ask, what would have happened if the first two servants had traded with their master's money, but things hadn't worked out so well, and they had only made a little money or, even worse, what if they'd *lost* money? How would the master have treated them then? What if the first two had lost money, but the third had returned the same amount to his master…would the master's response have been any different?

I guess we'll never know, because that's not the way the story goes. What's important to recognize, though, is that all three of them were given a task that involved some degree of risk. All of them risked disappointing their master. The difference between them was that the first two at least tried to make something good happen; the third didn't even try. For the third, at least, covering his own butt seemed to be his primary concern. And that's exactly, of course, what ended up getting him in trouble. The first two appear to have been motivated by a desire to please their master. The third appears to be concerned with avoiding his master's anger, with playing it safe. And that difference ends up being huge.

What I think this story teaches us loud and clear is this: life involves risk. Life without risk is a myth, and a dangerous one at that.

For anything good to happen usually requires some amount of risk. "Nothing ventured, nothing gained," goes the old saying, meaning that if you don't try to make something good happen, it most likely won't. Even more important, however, and more dangerous, is the mistake of thinking that it's possible to play it safe all the time, and never experience anything bad.

This doesn't mean that we're supposed to be irresponsible, or to take unnecessary risks. That's just as stupid and dangerous as being afraid to take any risk. The point is that each of us has the capacity to use our talents and our gifts to make something good happen. In order for that to take place, however, we're each going to have to put ourselves on the line from time to time.

Nobody likes getting yelled at on the field for making a mistake. But I bet that if I asked the coaches whether they'd rather have you play hard, take some risks and make mistakes, or play it safe and not give 100%, ten times out of ten they'd say they'd rather see you go all out and make mistakes, than hold back and play it safe.

And if you think this is true on the playing field, you've got to understand how true it is in the military. This profession, this way of serving your country is full of risk. It doesn't take a rocket scientist to figure that out. We are called upon to perform risky tasks, in dangerous and challenging circumstances, and the stakes are often incredibly high. Each of us must learn how to find the right balance between taking calculated risks, and mitigating them.

You will find, I'm sorry to say, many officers whose sole goal appears to be to not make any mistakes. There are too many officers who weigh each decision based on how it might affect their career if something goes wrong. Don't be one of them. They are those, "cold and timid souls" Teddy Roosevelt talks about, who are afraid to take chances because they're afraid of failing. You did not make this team by playing it safe. You made it by putting out, day in and day out. Sometimes you've been successful, sometimes you haven't. The coaches don't make it easy for you when you fail. But where would you be if you didn't even try? You wouldn't be here, that's for sure.

In aviation, we spend a lot of time mitigating risks, making it as safe as possible. There is, of course, one way to make flying absolutely safe: don't fly. Obviously, that's not a legitimate option. So we devote ourselves to learning our craft as carefully as possible, practicing it as often and hard as possible, and then when the time comes, we trust our training, preparation, abilities, and teammates, and go as hard and fast as we can to accomplish the mission.

Sounds a lot like football, doesn't it?

Each of you has something to offer. Your coaches and your teammates are counting on you to bring it to the game. If you screw up, pick yourself up and determine to do it better next time. But don't hold back. That's the biggest mistake of all.

Game Wrap:

It was indeed a tough day for Navy, on both sides of the ball.

Junior slot back Shun White and Junior fullback Eric Kettani both demonstrated that they could be as dangerous running the ball as their senior counterparts, but in the end Navy simply could not keep up with a potent Wake Forest offense that capitalized on Navy mistakes.

Kaipo left the game late in the second quarter with a neck injury, and Wake Forest managed to score ten quick points to end the first half. A total of three Navy turnovers allowed Wake Forest to amass a lead that the Mids could not overcome, although at one point they had closed the gap to three.

How the rest of the season would go was still very much in the air.

Final Score: Navy 24 – Wake Forest 44

Week Eight:
Navy vs. University of Delaware

✦

Senior slotback Zerbin Singleton

Someone once made the observation that, "Navy's had the same guys on their team for the last hundred years."

Which is to say that while Navy's football program has experienced its glory years—a National Championship in 1926, Heisman trophy winners in 1960 and 1963—and its years of drought—a cumulative record of 11-48 between 1998 and 2002—what has remained consistent throughout the 128-year history of Navy football is the character and determination of its players.

The other, more quantifiable quality about Navy that has changed little over the years is the size of the players. In 1927 the average weight of the Navy football players was 173 pounds. In 1964, the year after Roger Staubach won his Heisman Trophy, the average weight was 197. On the 2007 Navy team, the average weight was 205 pounds. That's an increase of only about 18 percent over the past eighty years.

To really appreciate the current difference in size between Navy and other BCS Division teams, look at how the 2007 Navy and Notre Dame teams stacked up against each other: the average weight of the Navy starting offensive players was 230, and 220 for the defensive starters. The average weight of Notre Dame's starting offense was 265, and 237 for the defense. But consider this: the average weight of Notre Dame's offensive line was 305 pounds; the average weight of Navy's defensive line was 261! Notre Dame had five offensive linemen that exceeded 300 pounds; Navy had none.

What the Midshipmen lack in size, though, they make up for in spirit, and in heart. And nobody personified this better than senior slot back Zerbin Singleton.

Zerb was the heart and soul of the 2007 team. As if his play on the field wasn't inspirational enough—at this point in the season he was the team's third leading receiver and had accumulated 517 all-purpose yards and was a ferocious blocker—it was the story of his life that earned him the respect of everyone who knew him, and a reputation as a leader on and off the field, and as a truly special human being.

When Zerb was only eleven, his mother was shot and incarcerated, and Zerb was sent to the Atlanta area to live with cousins. It was they, says Zerb, who instilled in him the faith and the values that became the foundation of his character. As a senior in high school, Zerb met his biological father for the first time in his life. A standout football player in high school, Zerb was nonetheless told by Georgia Tech that he was too small to play Division I football.

He was accepted to both the Air Force and Naval Academies, and, according to sportscaster Bob Socci, chose Navy because someone asked him, as an aspiring pilot, "Would you rather take off and land on land, or land (when it's) pitch black at night, on a carrier tilting from side to side?" Shortly before he was to report for Plebe Summer, however, Zerb's car was hit head on by a drunk driver, and he suffered a broken collarbone, which made him medically ineligible to report. He applied again, and was accepted, and began his Naval Academy career a year later. Within a few months, his world was again rocked by tragedy when his biological father committed suicide.

Without a doubt, Zerb had more reason than most people to be bitter, or discouraged, or understandably distracted from pursuing his dreams.

Zerb is none of these.

He majored in Aerospace Engineering—one of the most difficult majors offered at the Naval Academy—and accumulated a GPA of over 3.2. He was named Brigade Commander—the position of highest rank and responsibility for Midshipmen—for the second semester of his senior year, and was subsequently commissioned as a Second Lieutenant in the United States Marine Corps, and selected for Naval Flight Training. He aspires to be an astronaut.

In the locker room and on the field, Zerb gave off more energy than a nuclear reaction. Before each game Zerb would be, literally, bouncing off the other players in the locker room, charging up the team with shouts of, "C'mon, baby! These guys'll never know what hit 'em! Let's go, baby!" His contribution to the team's pre-game prayer was something I looked forward to every week, when he would invariably quote Psalm 27: "The Lord is my light and my salvation; whom shall I fear? The Lord is the stronghold of my life; of whom shall I be afraid?"

On the field, Zerb wasn't afraid of anybody! As a blocker, he was probably more responsible for big plays than anybody on the team. With the ball, he was just as likely to be airborne, parallel to the ground, soaring toward the end zone, as he was plowing into a wall of defenders that outweighed him by 150 pounds each!

Zerb Singleton will not play pro football, nor did he play for a national championship team. As far as I know, he didn't set any records at Navy. And yet by the end of the season he would be recognized as one of the country's most outstanding college football players, receiving the Disney Wide World of Sports Spirit Award, given each year to college football's most inspirational figure, and the FedExOrange Bowl – FWAA Courage Award, for displaying courage on or off the field, or overcoming hardship.

Zerb was, without a doubt, the heart and soul of the 2007 team. And everybody who knew him will tell you exactly the same thing.

You are writing your own Story.
2 Samuel 11-12

Regardless of what religious background you come from, or how well you know the Bible, you've probably all at least heard of a guy named David. He's the guy who, as a boy, killed the great warrior giant Goliath, and he later became the great King of Israel. David is held up as one of the great heroes of the Bible, and in fact the Bible refers to him as, "a man after God's own heart."

"A man after God's own heart." That's quite a thing to be said about somebody, isn't it? If you're a person of faith, that's about the highest compliment that can be paid to somebody. So David was this legendary hero, a great king, a famous warrior, and a man after God's own heart. Not a bad resume, eh?

But here's the thing: David did some pretty bad things, and one in particular stands out as something that we might be tempted to call "unforgivable." Very briefly, what he did was this: his armies were out to battle one springtime, and King David was lounging around in his castle. We don't know why he wasn't out leading his troops. But one evening he saw this incredibly beautiful woman bathing. He asked who she was, and was told that her name was Bathsheba, and that she was the wife of one of David's soldiers, who was away fighting. David sent for her—don't forget, he was the king, and could pretty much have everything he wanted—and they had sex, and she got pregnant.

So to try and cover things up, David sent for her husband—his name was Uriah—and brought Uriah to his castle, and told Uriah to take a break, go home and enjoy his wife before he went back to the fight. Obviously, David was assuming that after Uriah had been home for a day or two, everybody would assume that it was Uriah who had made his wife pregnant.

But Uriah refused to go home. He said to David, "How can I go home, and sleep in my own bed, and enjoy my own wife, when my soldiers are out in the field suffering and fighting?" Uriah, apparently, was a pretty honorable guy. So the next night David got him drunk and tried to send him home, but still Uriah refused to go.

Finally, David sent Uriah back to the battle, and sent a message to his commander to put Uriah in the middle of the worst fighting, and make sure that he got killed. And that's what happened. Uriah died in the fighting, and David took Bathsheba as his own wife.

Now, I don't know about you, but I don't know that I've ever heard of anything more underhanded, back-stabbing, and dishonorable than what David did to Uriah, a completely innocent and honorable man, who happened to have a beautiful wife. I promise you, guys, that when you get to the fleet, you will encounter, in one way or another, the struggles of married men and women when one of them goes to war, or on deployment. It's a story that's been repeated for as long as men and women have gone off to fight and left their wives and husbands and families at home. And it is always a painful, heart-breaking mess.

But, more to the point, how can David, who did such a terrible thing, be considered a hero, and a "man after God's own heart?"

Well, to make any sense out of things, we have to look at the entire story of David's life, and particularly at what he did once he had realized what a terrible thing he had done. And, incidentally, it took somebody else to point out to him how awful his actions were. But, to David's credit, he accepted responsibility for his actions, and confessed his sins to God. And the Bible says that God forgave David. God made David pay some pretty serious consequences—both in the short term and in the long term—but because David was willing to admit that what he had done was wrong, and asked for God's forgiveness, and, we assume, devoted himself to not repeating his mistake, he was able to get his life back on track, and in the end to earn the approval of God and of history.

Here's why I think this story is important: last week, I encouraged you to not be afraid to make mistakes. But the reality is that we will *all* make mistakes, at various points in our lives—even the "best" of us, even David, a "man after God's own heart." So part of any discussion about making mistakes has to be how do we handle ourselves when we *do*, in fact, make a mistake…even a big one?

This is a much bigger question than I'm going to try and answer here, but for now what I hope you'll remember is this: one element of a person's character is making the best decisions we can. An equally important element of character, though, is learning to pick ourselves up, recover from our mistakes, do what we can to make them right, and then move on, determined not to repeat the same mistakes twice. That is the only way to avoid being overwhelmed by guilt and fear, or to repeat our mistakes, which is one sign of true stupidity.

What made David a man after God's own heart is the story of his *entire life*, not his individual mistakes or triumphs.

What kind of story is your life telling? What I want you to recognize is that the story that your life tells is much more than a simple tally of what you did "right", and what you did "wrong." Your lives can't be broken down into post-game stat sheets, like the coaches look at after each game. Those may be some of the events in your life, but *who you are* is about much more than that! Who you are isn't about successes or failures, but about character, and integrity, attitude and persistence, courage and commitment. I'm not suggesting that the successes and failures aren't important…they are. But they don't tell the whole story! Not by a long shot.

I don't want to embarrass Zerb here, but he's a great example of what I'm talking about. Zerb's a good football player. We all know that. But what makes Zerb really special, what has earned him all of our admiration and respect is *who he is*, on and off the field. We've all heard his story—the challenges and hardships he's encountered and overcome in his life. And we all know his aspirations! Does anybody who knows him doubt for a minute that Zerb will eventually be an astronaut? I'd bet on the Superintendent giving permission for Plebes to wear civilian clothes to class before I'd bet against Zerb!

What makes Zerb so special is the *entire story* of his life, up to this point. Yeah, he's good on the field, but it's about a whole lot more than that, as well. We see his heart when he runs the ball, but we also see it in the Brigade, in the locker room, and in his family life. Zerb is writing his own story; and he's refused to let the circumstances of his life dictate the story that it tells.

Think back to Teddy Roosevelt's words from the "Man in the Arena": *who errs and comes short again and again…*" Nobody whom we consider to be a success has lived a life free of failure, and in fact most of our greatest heroes have endured the greatest failures. George Washington lost a *lot* of battles, and was on the verge of losing the entire war a number of times. But he came through when it counted, and is remembered not just as a great general, but as the "Father of our country." Abraham Lincoln lost more elections than he won, but he never quit, and when he did win, he made the most of it.

I want to tell you a story about a guy you've never heard of, and you probably never will, except for here. His name is Mike, and he was a flight mechanic in the Coast Guard back when I was a Coastie helicopter pilot. One night we were conducting a MEDEVAC flight from an island off the Los Angeles coast, and, through a strange chain of events, Mike was pulled out the cabin door of the helicopter we were flying, in midair. He was wearing a gunner's belt, which is a strap that was secured around his waist and attached to the helo, but Mike was hanging underneath the helicopter, upside down, at night, in the clouds, going about one hundred twenty miles an hour, about a thousand feet over the Pacific Ocean. And in addition, we didn't know if we had any aircraft damage or not. I know this is the case, because I was the pilot in command. And I tell you what, fellas…they don't teach you in flight school what to do when stuff like this happens. Oh, and by the way, I was a relatively new Aircraft Commander, and had only been flying this model of helicopter for a few months.

At that moment, all the elements were there for things to go very, very badly. But what happened was this: Mike kept his cool. He realized that his ICS—the communication chord that allowed him to talk to the rest of the crew—was still attached to his helmet, and that he could still talk to me. And after yelling at me to "slow the [blank] down!" he did, in fact, start to talk to me. I slowed down, he calmed down, and we started to work out a solution. Eventually, we were able to pull into a hover about twenty-five feet over the water, lower the rescue hoist hook to where Mike could grab it, and he was able to hold on while we pulled him back up to the cabin door, and he pulled himself back into the cabin.

I want to tell you that the guy who was primarily responsible for Mike's safe rescue was Mike himself. He refused to give in to some pretty lousy circumstances, and he, himself, wrote his own story.

I've said this before, and I'll say it many times again: we don't get to choose the circumstances of our lives. But it is always up to us to decide how we respond to whatever circumstances we are confronted with. David, Zerb, Mike, the list goes on and on of people who refused to let their failures define or discourage them, and who took responsibility for writing their own stories.

There will be some successes this game, there will be some mistakes. Recognize, though, that every play is a part of a larger story—the game. Each game is part of a larger season, and this season is just a part of a much larger story of your preparation as officers of Sailors and Marines…and so it goes, on and on. You are writing your own personal story as well. It's early, but what you are writing now will impact the way your story unfolds from here on. Will it, in the end, be about people who allowed their lives to be defined by the ups and downs of fate? Or will your story be about a man after God's own heart?

Game Wrap:

"Delaware? You lost to Delaware?? I didn't even know they had a football team!"

That's how a friend of mine greeted me on the phone the week following this game. I suspect a lot of Navy players and fans got similar responses. Delaware does, in fact, have a football team, and it happens to be one of the top teams in its division of college football. That division, however, is the Football Championship Subdivision, formerly known as Division I-AA, which accounts for why it's not very well known, and why there was such shock at Navy's loss.

I'm also pretty sure that the second-most commonly asked question was, *"How do you score fifty-two points and* lose???*"*

The answer, of course, is that you let the other team score fifty-nine.

In a "normal" college football season, this game might qualify as a "wild one." In the context of Navy's season, however, it was more like, "just another game." The 111 total points scored was the most points scored in a Navy game since 1919. (True to form for this season, however, that record would not last long.) And while Navy racked up 509 yards of total offense, Delaware managed to accumulate 581.

Two Navy fumbles killed drives that might have made all the difference, as the offense scored on all but one of its other possessions. Kaipo, Senior fullback Adam Ballard, Junior fullback Eric Kettani, and Senior slotback Reggie Campbell all rushed for touchdowns, while Junior quarterback Jarod Bryant relieved Kaipo in the third quarter, and completed eight of eleven attempts for 126 yards, in addition to rushing for twenty-five yards and one touchdown. After forcing two punts early in the game, Navy's defense gave up 434 passing yards, including four touchdowns.

There's no question that the loss was a shock and a disappointment to the team. And with two of their biggest challenges of the season still ahead of them—Notre Dame and Army—how they bounced back from this one would say a lot about their character as a team.

Final Score: Navy 52 – Delaware 59

WEEK NINE:
Navy @ Notre Dame

✦

Navy's defense overwhelms Notre Dame's Armando Allen

"The Streak."

It was impossible to avoid the term, or the topic, as Navy prepared to travel to Notre Dame for the eighty-first meeting between the two schools.

The streak, of course, was Navy's NCAA-record forty-three straight losses to the Fighting Irish, a streak that dated back to 1963, when Navy last beat Notre Dame, led by a Heisman Trophy-winning quarterback named Roger Staubach. Were it not for the history shared by these two programs, it could be argued that the two schools shouldn't even be playing each other any more. (The fascinating history between the Navy and Notre Dame football programs, however, all but guarantees that the two schools will, in fact, continue to play each other. But that's a different story…).

What made this year's game a bit more interesting, however, had little to do with Navy, but with the fact that Notre Dame was suffering through its worst season in years, entering the game with a record of one-and-seven. "If Navy's ever going to beat Notre Dame, this is the year," was a common refrain. Nevertheless, most predictions gave the Irish a solid advantage, referring to Navy's struggling defense, and the fact that Notre Dame had had two weeks to prepare for the Midshipmen. And they were still, after all, Notre Dame.

It is hard to describe the feeling of walking through the tunnel of Notre Dame Stadium—"The House that Rockne Built"—and onto the field for the first time. As if the history that seems to permeate the structure itself isn't enough, the banners hanging the length of the tunnel remind you: seven Heisman Trophies, thirteen National Championships. The bricks themselves echo names like Joe Montana, Jerome Bettis, Lou Holtz, Ara Parseghian, and of course, Knute Rockne.

In addition to the history of the place, two things struck me most on my first trip to South Bend. The first was the simplicity of the playing field. The stadium is a two-tiered bowl, surrounding a green grass field, with simple white lines. That's it. No design painted in the end zones, no artwork at the 50-yard line, no space-age looking architecture, no advertisements adorning the walls. Everything about the stadium conveys one simple message: nothing matters here except Notre Dame football.

My second impression was how friendly and hospitable our Notre Dame hosts were. Without exception, the volunteers who seemed to be everywhere greeted us with a smile and a genuine, "Welcome to Notre Dame! We're glad you're here." I suppose they're used to saying that, knowing full well that their football team is about to eat your football team for lunch. But even this year, their gracious and welcoming demeanor seemed undimmed by the painful season they were enduring. I will admit to having harbored some less-than-generous thoughts about the Fighting Irish. I am, after all, a Pac-Ten fan. But I came away from that weekend with a new appreciation for Notre Dame and their fans.

Of course, that doesn't mean I didn't want to crush them.

Saturday, November 3, 2007 was irrefutable proof that God is a college football fan. It was a glorious fall day, the campus was radiant in the brilliant orange and yellow and red of autumn, and the crowd was awash in the blue and gold that Navy and Notre Dame football share, and of course the green of the Irish.

Shortly after the team arrived at the stadium, while the players carried out their carefully choreographed pre-game preparations, I set out on two errands. The first was to take a photo of myself and Touchdown Jesus. This was accomplished with relative ease, since there were plenty of other folks there doing the same thing.

The second was to find "the Grotto," the existence of which I had only learned about the night before, but which I had promised the team I would visit. The Grotto, which was built on the Notre Dame campus in 1896, is a replica of the original Grotto of Our Lady in Lourdes, France. Throughout its history it has been a favorite place of worship, petition and reflection for the Notre Dame faithful. This includes, of course, football fans.

I found the grotto, and even though I didn't do exactly what I had said I would do, the trip was worth it...

A Personal Prayer

Every week, as I prepare to stand before you and offer you my thoughts and reflections, I try to find a message that applies to you on the field and off, and is relevant to you as football players, future leaders of Sailors and Marines, and young men of character and integrity. The extent to which I'm successful in that is up to you to judge, not me.

And so this week, I chose the story from Scripture that I wanted to tell you, thought about what I wanted to say to you, and began to formulate a way to make it meaningful and effective for you in this morning's devotion.

And then, late last night, I set it aside.

For whatever reason, it didn't feel right. It felt forced, out of place, and so I'll save it for another day. Instead, I just want to share my own personal thoughts about being here with you, in this place, on this day.

I'll start with a confession, because they say that confession is good for the soul.

As hard as I try to *not* make this a priority when I talk to you, the simple and honest truth is that I want to say something that will help you win. Like each of you, I'm a competitor, and I want to win.

The reality, though, is that I can't help you win, nor is that what I'm here for. You are the guys on the field, you are the ones who will bear the burden of defeat, or wear the laurels of victory. Now don't get me wrong, nothing's going to stop me from throwing plenty of fourth-

and-short prayers God's way, but in the end, the game is yours to play, yours to win or lose. My job is to be there on the sidelines with you.

Now, one of the things that we who wear the uniforms of our country share is that we don't like to be on the sidelines. We are doers, not watchers. We are people who want to be a part of the action; we want to do something, and do something that matters. When I was a helicopter pilot in the Coast Guard I loved the idea of swooping down in my bright orange helicopter and saving the day.

When I became a chaplain, it took me a while to get used to the idea that I wasn't an operator any more. It wasn't my job to ride in and save the day; it was my job to support and care for the men and women who did.

What I've found, though, is this: when you make yourself available to help people, you end up being blessed in ways you could never imagine. One of the things I appreciate most about the Marines is that once you demonstrate that, as a chaplain, you really care about them, and are willing to simply be there with them and for them, you no longer are *a* chaplain; you are *their* chaplain. And they will do anything for you. That is a humbling and gratifying feeling.

Whatever your role is on this team, you need to know that it's important, and you wouldn't be sitting here in this room if you didn't have something to offer to the team, and to the mission. Even if you never set foot on the field, you have earned the right to be here, and there is a way for you to contribute. Never underestimate the impact that a word of encouragement can have on a teammate. Don't underestimate how much your energy level on the sidelines can motivate and inspire your teammates on the field. Whatever your role is at any given time, you have something to offer.

Last night, at dinner, [Navy Athletic Director] Chet Gladchuck told us a story, and I want to tell it to you:

Back in the 90's, Chet was AD at Boston College. For the first time in many years, BC and Notre Dame played each other. And Notre Dame crushed them, 54-7. Absolutely killed them. And then, as if to rub salt in the wound, in the fourth quarter, Notre Dame kicked an onside kick, and got the ball back yet again.

BC's coach that year was Tom Coughlin…you may remember him as the guy who coached the Giants to last year's Super Bowl. Anyway, Coach Coughlin was absolutely livid that Lou Holtz, then coaching the Irish, would do something as grandstanding and unsportsmanlike as that. He was so furious that he refused to walk over and shake Holtz's hand after the game.

According to Chet, Coughlin could have gone to the Giants that year, but instead he stayed at Boston College, and he did it for one reason: he vowed to beat Lou Holtz and Notre Dame.

Okay, flash forward to the next season. Notre Dame is in the hunt for the national championship. The only school standing in their way is Florida State, who was also undefeated, and making a claim on the title. If the Irish could beat Florida State, it was smooth sailing from there, with only lowly Boston College and Army between them and their destiny as National Champions.

Here on the Notre Dame campus, there's a shrine that's referred to as "the Grotto," and it's a place of prayer and devotion, where people often light candles as a part of their prayer practices. The week before the Florida State game, there were something like 10,000 candles lit in the Grotto. In fact, Sports Illustrated carried a photo of the Grotto in their issue the following week, and the place looked like it was on fire. Well, Notre Dame beat Florida State that week in a thrilling game that came down to the final play, and their National Championship looked like a lock.

The next week the Irish hosted Boston College; by all accounts it was to be an easy win for the Irish. Some time before the game, Tom Coughlin decided to make a trek to the Grotto and say a prayer. Apparently, he was the only one there, and there were, like, ten candles lit. Nobody gave BC a prayer, and apparently the Irish fans weren't taking this game particularly seriously. But Coach Coughlin nonetheless lit a candle, and began to pray. And in a couple minutes, Lou Holtz shows up. They look at each other; neither of them says a word. Lou lights his candle and starts to pray. After a little bit, Coach Holtz got up and left. When he was gone, Coach Coughlin decided to light another candle, just to be sure. And then, as he walked out, he took a quick look around, made sure that nobody was looking…and he blew out Lou Holtz's candle.

Boston College beat Notre Dame that day on a last second field goal…according to Chet, it was the ugliest kick he'd ever seen. But, miraculously, it went through, and BC had spoiled Notre Dame's championship hopes. The following year, Coach Coughlin left BC for the NFL.

Is this a true story? I don't know. But it doesn't matter. What I want you to remember is that this is college football, and anything can happen. Today is today, and it's all that matters. Someday, Lieutenant Colonel Benson and Commander Kennedy and Captain Hamilton [the team's active duty officer representatives] and I will welcome you onto the active duty Navy and Marine Corps team. For now, though, you've welcomed us onto your team.

I'll be there on the sidelines doing my part, and today, my part will include saying a prayer for each of you at some point during the game. That's my promise to you: I will pray for each one of you, by name, at some point during the game. That's the role I can play, it's a way for me to contribute, and I want you to know I'll be doing it.

And, before the game, if I get a chance, I may also wander over to the Grotto, and see if I can blow out Charlie Weiss's candle...

[After I said this, I glanced over at Coach Johnson. It was the only time during a pre-game meal I saw him smile.]

Game Wrap:

Pandemonium.

That's the only word that comes close to describing the scene on the Navy sidelines and the Midshipmen cheering section as Navy's defense—led by linebacker Irv Spencer and lineman Michael Walsh—swarmed Notre Dame running back Travis Thomas short of the end zone on fourth and goal in the third overtime, and the scoreboard told the final story: the streak was over.

The players swarmed the field. The Midshipmen in the stands swarmed each other. Back in Bancroft Hall in Annapolis, Mids burst from their rooms, swarming the halls and spilling out onto the huge courtyard known as Tecumseh Court, or "T-Court" and erupting in a spontaneous party that lasted for hours. My first instinct was to take a photo of the scoreboard. Then, I just tried to take it all in. It was too much.

At one point, I saw Navy assistant coach Danny O'Rourke leaping onto a pile of players, blood streaming down his face from a gash in his head. I'm not sure he'd even felt a thing.

Aside from the simple fact of Navy's beating Notre Dame for the first time in forty-four years, the game included all the elements of a classic college football contest: lots of scoring, dramatic defensive stands, three overtimes, and the outcome of the game coming down to the final play—fourth and goal from the one yard line...twice! The game was peppered with performances and plays that were heart-stopping and nothing short of valiant: Defensive End Chris Kuhar-Pitters was named the National Defensive Player of the Week for plays like his fumble recovery and touchdown to give Navy the lead *in the fourth quarter; linebacker Ram Vela's spectacular leaping rush resulted in a sack of Irish quarterback Evan Sharpley and the end of a late game Irish drive, forcing the game into overtime; Kaipo and Reggie Campbell hooked up not only to score the go-ahead touchdown in the third overtime, but then again on the next play for what turned out to be the winning two-point conversion; and the battered but unrelenting Navy defense refused to quit time and time again, finally ending the forty-three game losing streak with their heroic goal-line stand, which included having to replay the final fourth and goal after being called for pass interference.*

Even many of the Notre Dame fans seemed to appreciate that something historic had happened. Displaying remarkable sportsmanship, words of "congratulations" were offered by Irish supporters from up in the press box to down on the field. Players from both teams stood respectfully for each other's Alma Maters after the game, both of which were sung loudly and passionately by the respective student sections.

In the locker room following the game, Commandant of Midshipmen Captain Margaret Klein congratulated the team by cancelling classes the following Monday for the entire Brigade of Midshipmen. When the Mids arrived back at the Academy around midnight, the entire Brigade was waiting for them in T-Court, and the party started up all over again.

Final Score: Navy 46 – Notre Dame 44 (3OT)

Week Ten:
Navy @ University of North Texas

◆

Sophomore linebacker Ram Vela's "Superman" rush on Notre Dame quarterback Evan Sharpley

Navy was still glowing in the aftermath of their historic win over Notre Dame. They were one game away from being able to accept an invitation to play in the San Diego Poinsettia Bowl. They boasted the nation's best rushing offense, and they were three-and-one on the road so far this year.

North Texas, on the other hand, was suffering through one of its worst seasons ever. Their record was one-and-seven, which put them second from the bottom of the Sun Belt Conference. Their defense was statistically one of the worst in the nation.

In other words, conditions were perfect for an upset.

With twenty-seven players on its roster from Texas, Navy had a sizeable cheering section at the Mean Green's Fouts Stadium. (Even I had fans in the stands...my brother in law and two nieces!) I don't think anybody there, however, was prepared for what was about to take place...

Remembering Goliath
1 Samuel 17

I don't know if the North Texas football team has a chaplain, but if they did, and I were him, here's what I'd tell them:

I'd tell the story of David and Goliath.

Now I know you've all heard that story before, but let me refresh your memory briefly. There was a war going on between the Israelites and the Philistines. Both camps were gathered on either side of a valley: the valley of Elah. And one day there walks out into the valley a monster of a man, a Philistine giant named Goliath. He stood between seven and nine feet tall. The head of his spear alone weighed 19 pounds! And he called out to the Israelites that he would fight their best warrior, one on one, and whichever warrior won, then that side would win the battle and the other army would be their servants.

Basically, Goliath was calling out Israel, and saying, Look, send out your best man, and we'll fight it out, and settle this thing quickly. Otherwise, we'll bring this battle to you until you're *all* dead.

Israel didn't have anybody to send up against this monster, and they were terrified and ready to just surrender.

Through a strange chain of events, a shepherd boy named David came to Israel's camp. This is the same David we talked about a couple weeks ago, except that this was before anybody knew who he was. David's older brothers were soldiers in Israel's army, and when David saw what was happening, he wondered why Israel was afraid to send out someone to face Goliath. So David said to the King, "Don't worry; I'll go fight him. I'm a shepherd, and I'm used to fighting lions and bears to protect my sheep. I'm not afraid of this guy."

So out David walks the next morning, into the valley, to face Goliath, one on one. First Goliath laughs at him, and then he gets angry, because he thinks the Israelites are mocking him. It's not hard to see why. David was just a boy, and he wasn't wearing any armor or apparently carrying any weapons. So Goliath starts making his approach, and David not only stands his ground, but starts running *toward* Goliath! David takes a rock, puts it in his sling and flings it at Goliath, hitting him so hard that the rock embeds itself in the giant's forehead, and that was all she wrote. Goliath fell to the ground, and David cut off his head with his own sword.

This is, of course, the classic story of the underdog taking on the overwhelming favorite, against all the odds, but through faith and courage, emerging victorious. In our case, we're usually David, and the other team is Goliath.

But I tell you what, guys. This week, as far as North Texas is concerned, we're Goliath, and they're David. We're the Division One guys, coming to town in our fancy Nike uniforms fresh off our historic upset of Notre Dame, with all of the publicity and hoopla.

And all of the odds.

I guarantee that they're going to come after us with a vengeance. Because they have absolutely nothing to lose. They see us as the cocky giant expecting an easy victory, and themselves as the faithful, courageous underdogs who are going to teach the big boys from the East a lesson about Texas football, no matter what division we're talking about.

The thing about the story of David and Goliath, though, is this: Goliath shouldn't have lost. If you take the element of God's favor toward David out of the equation—which of course you can't do with the Bible, but let's just do it anyway, for a minute—Goliath did not have to lose. He *shouldn't* have lost! He had everything in his favor.

But he got cocky. He got careless and complacent. And he got caught by surprise, and it cost him.

If *attitude, heart* and *focus* are the keys to winning—as we've said they are—then complacency, arrogance and carelessness are the keys to losing. And that's exactly what they are counting on to happen to us today. Whether or not that happens is entirely up to you.

Like I've said again and again this season, the things I'm talking about are important and true about a lot more than football.

Two weeks ago, I told you the story about my flight mechanic, Mike, who was primarily responsible for his own rescue. Next week, I'm going to tell you another side of that story—my side. And how another story quite literally, I believe, saved my life that night. Saved all our lives. For now, though, I want to remind you of that story because it's a great example of how you will encounter situations in your life that you never dreamed of, and that nobody could have prepared you for.

When you get the Fleet, whether it's in the field with your Marines or at sea with your Sailors or any other situation, you will *very* quickly find yourselves in situations where more things are happening all at the same time than you can keep track of, and all of them will be demanding—screaming for your attention. Chaos and confusion will threaten to overwhelm you, and you will have to learn to very quickly determine what is the most important element of any particular situation or moment, and force yourself to narrow your focus there. You will have to force yourself not to be distracted by a hundred other things all vying for your attention.

Of all the qualities that leadership demands, particularly in the military, one of the most critical is the ability to quickly determine what is the most important thing, and to focus on it, and it primarily. As one commander of mine told me once, "you have to learn to keep the main thing, the main thing."

Goliath forgot what was the main thing: winning the battle. He got caught up in appearances and expectations. He let his ego get in the way, and his emotions distracted him from his job. He assumed he knew how the fight was going to go, and consequently he lost the ability to react to unexpected circumstances. What got him was something he never saw coming. He let his guard down, and it cost him everything.

The Bible, and in fact most religious traditions that I'm aware of, recognize that life is full of distractions. And they teach us that discernment, focusing on the right thing at the right time is one of the keys to not getting swept away or blown off course. There is a time and a place for everything. Wisdom comes in learning to discern what is most important and necessary at any given time, and in being able to *focus* on that thing, knowing that there will be a time later for the other things.

I know last week was huge, and historic. We all do. But as frustrating as it may feel, that doesn't matter any more. Not right now. I know many of you are from Texas, and you have lots of friends and family here watching you. I know that with a win today we become bowl-eligible. I know you've got exams looming, and for the Firsties, Service Selection Night is coming up.

All of those things are important, and all of them will have their time. But this is not it. You have to be able to set all that aside, and recognize that there is *one thing* that demands your attention and your focus right now.

When you get to the Fleet, your ability to perform, to lead, and to succeed in your mission will depend on your ability to discern what is important, and focus on it. You will need to learn that skill earlier and better than most of your contemporaries. And today, right here and now, is the time to learn it, and to practice it.

In my mind, this is your primary challenge today: when you take the field, you have got to remember to keep the main thing, the main thing.

Game Wrap:

To call this game a "wild one" would be like referring to the sinking of the Titanic as "an unfortunate boating accident." This game was a shootout from the opening series, and initially it looked as if Navy was in big trouble. North Texas scored on its first possession, then recovered an on-side kick and scored again, before Navy even got to touch the ball! At one point late in the first quarter Navy was down 21-3. Before it was all over, I think every player in both lineups had scored, including both team trainers, the Backfield Judge and the head groundskeeper.

Now, my purpose in writing this book was not *to write a statistical recap of the season. But this game was just too crazy to pass up on the opportunity to offer the following game summary:*

- North Texas drove 73 yards in thirteen plays to score a touchdown.
- Surprising Navy with an on-side kick, NT drove 59 yards in five plays for another touchdown.
- Navy settled for a field goal on their first possession.
- NT again went 79 yards in eight plays for their third touchdown.
- Kaipo hit Tyree Barnes for a 41 yard touchdown.
- North Texas was forced to punt, and the first quarter ended with NT ahead 21-10.
- Navy promptly fumbled and NT recovered, scoring on the next play.
- Navy then drove 80 yards in seven plays for a touchdown.
- NT drove 60 yards in two plays for a touchdown.
- Navy drove 78 yards in two plays for a touchdown.
- NT drove 39 yards in two plays for a touchdown.
- Navy drove 57 yards in seven plays for a touchdown.
- NT drove 70 yards in two plays for a touchdown.
- Navy drove 68 yards in seven plays for a touchdown.

- NT was forced to punt, and Navy drove 50 yards in two plays for the final touchdown of the FIRST HALF, bringing the score to, um…let's see…add the ones, carry the two…Navy 45, North Texas 49.
- The second half looked like it would continue the pattern, with Navy taking the kickoff and driving 60 yards in nine plays for a touchdown.
- North Texas then threw an interception, allowing Navy to drive 80 yards in three plays for another touchdown. Navy never relinquished the lead after that.
- NT drove 59 yards in seven plays to score a touchdown.
- Navy drove 64 yards in three plays for a touchdown.
- NT threw another interception, but Navy couldn't capitalize and had to punt (yes, Navy actually had a punter, even though you didn't get to see him very often: senior Greg Veteto, a heck of a nice guy, but very bored for most of the season.)
- Starting the fourth quarter ahead 65-56, Navy again picked off a NT pass, but again had to punt.
- Navy's defense forced a safety, and then Reggie Campbell ran back the ensuing free kick 73 yards for a Navy touchdown.
- NT came back with a 71 yard, twelve play drive for a touchdown.

In the end, most of the scoreboard's lights had burned out, and bets were being offered on whether or not the Mean Green's basketball team would score as many points as their football team in their game later that night. Navy scored their most points since beating Colby (who?) 121-0 back in 1919, and ran for a school-record 572 yards, which certainly helped to cement their position as the nation's top rushing offense.

Final Score: Navy 74 – North Texas 62
This was the highest scoring regulation-time football game in NCAA Division I-A history.
With this win Navy became eligible to accept an invitation to play in the San Diego Poinsettia Bowl.

Week Eleven:
Navy vs. Northern Illinois University

♦

Senior slotback and team co-captain Reggie Campbell

If Zerb Singleton was the heart and soul of this Navy team, Reggie Campbell was its backbone. Chosen by his teammates as their offensive team captain, Reggie was as remarkable for his quiet, humble leadership off the field as he was for his explosive play on the field.

A three year letterman, Reggie accumulated numbers that not only established him as one of the most productive players in recent Navy history, but earned him attention on the national level, as he was invited to play in the 2008 Hula Bowl All-Star Game. He finished the season nineteenth in the NCAA in all-purpose yards, eleventh on Navy's career rush list, tied the NCAA record for most touchdowns in a bowl game with five against Colorado State in the 2005 Poinsettia Bowl, became the first player in school history to return two kickoffs for a touchdown in the same season (including a ninety-eight yard return he would make against Army the following week), and the most prolific kickoff return man in Navy history.

But, as is so often the case with Navy's players, the numbers only tell a portion of the story. At five feet six inches and 168 pounds, Reggie had to answer as many questions about his size as he did about his running. Off the field he was slow to speak, quick to smile, and never seemed to be in a hurry. In fact, a 2006 Washington Post article pointed out that he was such a slow walker that the other Midshipmen had to walk around him on the way to class. But his physical size belied the size of his spirit and his heart.

I don't recall Reggie missing a single practice because of injury. It wasn't because he wasn't hurt; as one of the key ball carriers in the nation's top rushing offense, Reggie took plenty of hits, usually by guys who outweighed him by a hundred pounds or more. I remember watching him take a hit in the Hula Bowl after the end of the season that sent him flying, it seemed, up to the second or third row of seats. But sure enough, back onto the field he trotted, and not too much later scored a touchdown.

To watch Reggie run from the perspective of the sidelines impressed upon me how quickly he could go from standing still to being a blur down the field. To watch his quiet leadership in the locker room, on the practice field, and in Bancroft Hall impressed upon me what a special young man he really was.

One of my all-time favorite movies is, "The Bridges at Toko-Ri," adapted from the novel by James Michener. At the end of the movie, after losing one of his fighter pilots and a rescue helicopter crew in a combat mission over North Korea, the Admiral sits on the flag bridge of his aircraft carrier and looks out to sea. Below him, the flight deck is busy preparing for the next round of aircraft launches. Out loud he ponders, "Where do we get such men? They leave this tiny ship and fly against the enemy. Then they must seek the ship, lost somewhere on the sea. And when they find it, they have to land upon its pitching deck. Where do we get such men?"

I suppose that for many people, that's a sappy, melodramatic monologue. But in my experience as a Chaplain to Marines and Sailors, that is perhaps the question that most often forms in my mind. Where do we continue to get such men and women? And even though our "combat missions" were football games, and the "enemy" was just another football team, time and time again I wondered how Navy managed to attract such devoted, talented, and fearless young men, who week after week faced teams that were bigger, stronger, and deeper than they were, but who nevertheless approached each contest with excitement and confidence, and a genuine expectation of winning. (I should note here that the women at Navy share the same strength of character, and the same indomitable spirit as the men.)

Reggie would be a leader on any team he played for. It just so happened that he was a leader of a team of leaders.

Learn, adapt, and overcome.
Jonah 2

Three weeks ago, I told you the story about my flight mechanic, Mike, who found himself one night in a very unexpected situation: hanging upside down underneath a helicopter one thousand feet over the Pacific Ocean. And yet in spite of the terrible circumstances in which he found himself, Mike kept his cool, and was largely responsible for affecting his own safe recovery.

Today, I want to tell you the rest of the story; the other side of the story. My side.

I mentioned that I was the Pilot in Command of that flight, and that I was a relatively young Aircraft Commander—which is the designation that the Coast Guard gives to pilots who are qualified to be in charge of flights and missions. In the Navy and Marine Corps we use the term "HAC", "Helicopter Aircraft Commander." Anyway, I was pretty young, and I hadn't been flying that particular model of helicopter for that long. In fact, nobody had. The HH-65A Dolphin was the Coast Guard's new helicopter, and we were still getting used to it, learning about it, figuring out what it did well, and what its limitations were.

So there I was, all of twenty-five or twenty-six years old, and responsible for the lives of a crew of three, plus two passengers—a doctor and the patient we were supposed to be MEDEVAC'ing—and a ten million dollar aircraft. And suddenly, one of my crew—one of the lives I was responsible for—was in dire jeopardy. To be perfectly honest, the first thought to clarify itself in my head was, "Holy sh**, this can't be happening."

I've learned that that's a pretty normal reaction in situations like those, but it was—and still is—a terrifying feeling. When that thought pops into your head, it's like a little warning light telling you, "This is not good! This is not good!" My stomach started to climb into my throat, my head begun to spin, and I started to feel hot all over.

Remember, now, that I'm at the flight controls, and we are in the clouds, at night, about one thousand feet over the Pacific Ocean, going about one hundred twenty miles an hour with possible aircraft damage, and my flight mechanic is hanging upside down under the helicopter. Oh, and by the way, I had absolutely no idea how strong the gunner's belt or its attachment point was, so I had no idea if or how long it would continue to hold Mike.

This was not a good time to panic.

But that's exactly what I wanted to do.

But at that moment—and this is the part of the story I remember more clearly than anything—I had an instant of clarity. Just a flash of recollection that popped into my head. And you know what I thought of?

A story.

I swear it's true. At that moment, in the middle of those circumstances, I remembered a story. Now, I didn't have to go through the entire story in my mind; just remembering the story was enough to clarify my thinking. But here's the story I remembered:

When I was in flight school, I'd met a Marine flight student. I don't even remember his name, but I remember, not too long after we'd both gotten our wings and gone our separate ways, hearing that he'd been in a crash. He was copilot on a CH-46 helicopter, and they were taking off from a ship at night. Now, you need to understand that even under perfect circumstances, flying to or from a ship at night is all business. There's not much room between you and the water, and when a helicopter meets the water, the results are never good.

And, in fact, that's what happened. Just as the aircraft was transitioning off the flight deck over the water—a critical time in a critical evolution—my friend looked down to re-tune one of the radios. In doing this, he took his eyes off the instruments, and therefore was no longer able to serve as a backup to the pilot who was flying. In that situation, you want both pilots concentrating on flying the aircraft because if something goes wrong, it's going to get a lot worse in a big hurry.

And it did. As I recall, the pilot got vertigo—not an unusual thing in that situation—and before he could recover—remember that he did not have his copilot backing him up—the helo was in the water. I don't remember if anybody died, but as I recall my friend suffered damage to his ears which made him unfit to fly again.

It had been a few years since I had first heard that story, and I had never forgotten it. And on the night when I found myself on the verge of panic, I believe that story saved my life. Here's why: if my first thought was, "Holy crap, I can't believe this is happening," my very next thought was, "I might lose Mike, but I am *not* going to fly my aircraft into the water and lose everybody else, too." I was kind of surprised at how quickly and clearly I was able to articulate it. I had to keep myself from dwelling on the possibility that I wouldn't be able to save my flight mechanic, but it was clear to me that if I didn't keep my head, the situation could get a lot worse, and a lot more tragic. And just that quickly, I was able to prioritize and re-focus my thoughts and emotions.

That moment of clarity allowed me to remember what was most important, and focus myself accordingly. Because I kept my head, and my copilot kept his, and everybody did everything absolutely right from that moment on, Mike was afforded the opportunity to bring about his own rescue.

Last week, guys, none of us expected to find ourselves down 21-3 in the first quarter.

And yet, not once, standing there on the sidelines, did I feel panicked. I don't know how you were feeling, but what I sensed was this realization that we were in a dogfight, and it was time to cinch up our chinstraps and dive in. You kept your focus, you dialed up your intensity, and you fought and clawed your way to a hard-earned win in an historic game. It might not have been a pretty win, but you got the job done because you refused to give up.

You may remember the story of Jonah from the Bible…the guy who's mostly remembered for getting swallowed by a big fish. But what really makes Jonah memorable is that he made some really big mistakes, some bad decisions that were the reason he ended up in the belly of a big fish. At that point, he could have despaired, he could have panicked, he could have given up. But he didn't.

One of the most memorable features of the Jonah story is the prayer that he offers up to God from inside the belly of the fish. When things couldn't possibly get any worse, Jonah remembered what was most important. He regained his perspective, and redirected his focus to what he knew to be true: that no matter what happened, his hope was with God. And the story makes it very clear that because Jonah did not give up hope, he was delivered. In spite of a string of bad—you could even say unfaithful—decisions, Jonah finally pulls himself together, remembers what's true and important, and gets back on task.

This season has not gone the way anybody predicted. It's been a roller coaster ride that has taken us in directions we did not expect, and put us in situations we did not anticipate. And yet, we keep fighting back. People keep writing us off, and we keep proving them wrong. The defense keeps getting criticized, and they keep coming up with big plays, while the offense keeps churning out the yards and getting us the points we need, and the special teams keep bouncing back from their mistakes with big plays. I told you a couple weeks ago you are writing your own story. I think you are writing a story you can be proud of.

If there is a signature characteristic of military service and leadership, I think it's never knowing for sure what you'll find yourself up against, and yet being ready and able to *adapt* and *overcome*. The worst mistake one can make is to panic, lose your composure, and abandon your training. There will always be a thousand things trying to capture your attention, distracting you from what is really important. You have got to learn to stay focused, keep your eye on the mission and the desired outcome, and throw yourself heart and soul into making that happen.

Seniors, this is your final home game. You've accomplished amazing, historic things since you've been playing for Navy. Show us how you did it. Take charge today, and show the younger guys what they need to do to keep the momentum, and the tradition, going strong.

Game Wrap:

Zerb Singleton and backup quarterback Jarod Bryant sparked another typical Navy offensive day, with Zerb scoring three touchdowns, and Bryant rushing for 140 yards and a score, as Navy racked up 419 total yards, 359 of them on the ground.

The defense began to assert itself as well, forcing four punts and picking off one pass, and holding NIU to one touchdown and one field goal in the second half.

For the Navy seniors, it was a great way to end their football careers at Navy-Marine Corps Stadium. It also was Navy's third consecutive win, giving them a good head of steam as they looked ahead to two weeks of preparation for the biggest game of the year: Army.

Final Score: Navy 35 – NIU 24

Week Twelve:
Navy vs. Army

◆

Senior fullback Adam Ballard

It's the hardest fought game in college football. Tears at the end, but buddies to the end, too.

This game is 10 times bigger than the Super Bowl.

The first thing they ask is, did you play football? The next thing they say is, did you beat Navy? It's not a game: It's a tradition.

Army-Navy rivalry brings out the best in college football.

The greatest rivalry in all of sports.

The sports pages and the airwaves burst with superlatives as Army-Navy week builds to a feverish pitch.

Photos from Iraq, Afghanistan, the Persian Gulf appear in countless emails of "GO ARMY – BEAT NAVY" banners hung from Saddam's palaces, and "BEAT ARMY" spelled out by Sailors across the flight deck of an aircraft carrier. One gets the sense that the entire nation—and much of the rest of the civilized world—is taking sides as this epic battle once again takes the world stage.

Of course, that's not the case, but you wouldn't know it if you lived within radio transmission distance of Annapolis, or West Point. And even though there are other famous rivalries in college football, this one is unique. Case in point: At the end of their very first day at the Academy, the Plebes sing, for the first time, their new Alma Mater, "Navy Blue and Gold." They will sing it at the end of every day of Plebe Summer, and countless times throughout their Academy and Navy careers. From the very first night, they end the song—as they will virtually every time they sing it for the rest of their lives—by thrusting their fists in the air and shouting, "BEAT ARMY!"

At Navy, there is one slogan that is consistent for all sports, one sentiment that permeates all aspects of Naval Academy life, one accomplishment that can redeem an otherwise disappointing season, one goal that unites all current Midshipmen with all former Midshipmen throughout all generations: BEAT ARMY.

Sitting proudly in the entrance to Memorial Hall on the Naval Academy campus since 2003 is the Commander-In-Chief's Trophy. Awarded every year to the service academy football team with the best record against the other service academies, Navy had dominated the service academy rivalry for the previous four years. With a win over Army, Navy would come within one win of tying Air Force for the most consecutive wins over both other service academies. And the senior class would graduate never having lost a game to another service academy.

Not that any of that really mattered.

In this rivalry, there's only one game that counts: this year's Army-Navy game.

Be strong and courageous
Joshua 1-2

One of the big mistakes people often seem to make when they read or think about the Bible, is that they assume that it's about these special, unique people that worked with God to make all these amazing things happen. If that's the way you understand the Bible, then it's a natural step to conclude, "but there's nothing special or amazing about me, and I've never talked to God, so I don't see how any of it is relevant to me." And that is, in fact, the way that many people look at the Bible: it's about other people, who are not like me, and therefore it's not really relevant for me.

Maybe that's the way some of you look at it. And like I said, that's understandable.

But I don't think it's correct.

Because if you really take the time to read the stories, you'll see very quickly that it is not amazing, special, superhuman people that God calls. Rather, it's regular people that God comes to, and God asks them to do something special. Often, the people are kind of knuckleheads, or they're looked down upon by society, or they're less than ethical. But what happens is this: God asks them to do something, and they say, simply, "Okay. Here I am. Send me." And with that simple agreement, they are on their way to doing amazing things. It is not amazing people who are the heroes of the Bible; it is normal people, who simply say "okay" to God's call, and who are then empowered to do amazing things.

When you think about it, our country is built on the same principle. It's not that we're a nation of superheroes that makes us what we are. Rather, we're a nation of common people, who step up to do uncommon things. It's been that way throughout our history, from the very beginning. And nowhere is it truer than in our military. With the possible exception of those times when we've had an active draft, our nation has always depended upon normal, so-called "common" people to step up, say, "Here I am...send me," and go on to do amazing, extraordinary things.

Each of you has taken that same step, made that same declaration: Here I am. Send me.

Do you ever wonder why the Army-Navy game is so huge? I mean, it's not like it's a game between two football powerhouses. That used to be true, but it hasn't been true for a long time. And yet it continues to be one of—if not *the*—quintessential sporting rivalry in our country.

Is it because of the tradition behind the game? The 108 years of history between these two teams? Maybe, and yet I'm not sure I buy that explanation completely either. Our culture has a notoriously short collective memory, and tradition seems to be less and less important to many people than short term gain.

There are no Heisman candidates, probably no All-Americans, no national championship implications—heck, it's been how many years since either team even broke into the Top 25?

So what is it about this game that seems to capture the national attention year after year?

I think it's this: I think that the people of our country—not just football or sports fans, but many, many people—deep down in our national consciousness, sense that something more than a football game is going on when these two teams take the field against each other. When they look at you, they see not just football players, but they see the young men—and by extension the young women, as well—who represent our country's hopes and dreams, and the best aspects of our national character: courage, honor, commitment, sacrifice, service. These are qualities that are talked about a lot, but the truth is that they are in seriously short supply in practice, in real life. But they see them in you. And it restores their hope that these things that we talk about as America's ideals are more than just words. They really exist.

People see how hard you play, how hard you try to win, regardless of the limitations that are placed upon you as Division One football programs, and they're impressed. But then they see the way that, as soon as the clock runs out and the game is over, you honor and respect each other. There is not some perfunctory shaking of hands and exchanging of high fives after this game; there are hugs, tears, congratulations and condolences that are real and deep and heartfelt. You know how much you want to win this game; so you know how badly it feels to lose it. As soon as the game is over, you are one team. You stand and sing each others' Alma Maters with true respect, because you know that as soon as you leave this field, the next time you meet each other may well be on the battlefield, fighting side by side.

I think the country sees that. And they are in awe.

They watch you, because they want to see these young men and women whom they have heard of, and about whom they have a sense that there is something truly special. And, perhaps, they have a sense that they are in debt to you, and how blessed they are—how blessed we all are—to have you, and others like you.

As corny as it may sound, they are thankful that there are young people like you not just out on the field, but out on the line. Out in places they don't even want to know about, doing things they pray they themselves, or their children, will never have to do. Perhaps they are looking to be reassured that there are, indeed, young men and women who are ready and willing to assume the responsibilities being passed down from those who have gone before you, and whose legacy you now make your own.

Which raises the following question: Are you ready? Do you, in fact, measure up?

You've all asked yourselves that question countless times throughout your lives and athletic careers. Am I ready? Can I get the job done? When the pressure is on, can I deliver? As people who wear the uniforms of our country, we ask ourselves similar questions: when the bullets start flying, how will I react? When people are counting on me to do something really difficult or dangerous, will I have what it takes?

There is not a man or woman who has ever served who has not asked him or herself that question. And I'm not sure we ever really know the answer, because the next time is always just around the corner.

But I believe one way to know you're ready is this: when your concern is not about yourself, but about the mission, and the well-being of the men and women around you...you're ready. If your concern is not, "How will *I* do?" but, "How will *we* do?" you're ready.

That's how I know that as a football team, you are ready.

Think back for a second to the first game of the season...my first message to you. Remember, "Into the fire?" Remember the firefighter rushing *up* the stairs, *into* the fire, while everybody else was rushing down the stairs, away from the flames? We can't read his mind, but we can read his actions. And regardless of what his mind was telling him, his actions were taking him toward the danger, into the fire. I suspect, however, that if we could read his mind, one of the things that we would hear repeated most frequently and most urgently would be, "My buddies are up there! They need me. I cannot let them down!" What drove him relentlessly up the stairs and into the fire is his awareness of his responsibility to them, his love for them. They were up there; he wanted to be there with them. He was not, under *any* circumstances, going to let his brothers and sisters down.

You are part of a brotherhood. It may have started on the football field, but it does not end there; not by a long shot. It's not even limited to those sitting in this room, or even the people you've played next to. It extends back 108 years, as long as there has been Navy football. You are a part of that now.

And in fact, the real brotherhood isn't based upon the football uniforms you wear, but upon the flag on the military uniforms you wear. The brotherhood includes the very guys you'll play against today, and whom you will join in the field in a few short months.

One of the most powerful symbols of the brotherhood and sisterhood of military service...something we all share, no matter what form our service takes, is the dog tag. I remember when I got my first set of dog tags, feeling that as of that moment, I was "in." I was a part of it all. My service was real.

Each of you, if you haven't already, will get your own set of dog tags at some point, and I suspect it will be a powerful moment for many of you, too. For now, though, I want to give you a reminder of the brotherhood you are already a part of. At each of your places, there's a dog tag. On one side of the tag is the emblem of the Naval Academy reminding you of where you started. On the other side, is a verse from the Bible, from the book of Joshua in the Hebrew Scriptures, that says, "Be strong and courageous; do not be frightened or dismayed. For the Lord your God is with you wherever you go."

The context for this quote is this: the Israelites were on the verge of entering the land that God had promised to their parents. But they had made one screw up after another, and so God delayed the time at which they would reach their destination. In that time their leader, Moses, had died, and had passed the mantle of responsibility to a new leader, a guy named Joshua. And Joshua was determined that they would not repeat the mistakes of the previous generation, and so he encouraged his people to trust in God to fulfill the promises that God had made. God tells Joshua to be strong and courageous for the challenges that lie ahead, and, in turn, Joshua encourages the people to be strong and courageous, for God is with them, and they have nothing to fear.

My hope is that this dog tag will be a symbol for you of the brotherhood of which you are a part, and of which you will *always* be a part. Not just on the field, but across services, and across time; not just back in time with those who have gone before, but forward in time, to those who will come after you. A reminder for you of how you stepped up when your country called and said, "Here I am, send me." My belief is that you are similarly bonded to God forever, and my prayer is that when God calls you, you will not be afraid to say, "Here I am, send me." Each of you will have to decide for yourself whether or not you believe that to be true.

For now, remember who you are, and whom you represent. Remember that you play not just for yourselves, but for those who have gone before. And you play for each other.

Be strong and courageous. Others have gone before you. Others will come after you. You are never alone.

Game Wrap:

The only thing more remarkable than the intensity with which these teams want to beat each other, is the respect that the two teams have for each other, and the bond they share as soon as the clock ticks off the final seconds. The hugs on the field are genuine, and there are tears on both sides of the field. It struck me as I watched them congratulate each other after the game, that some of the Navy tears—in addition to being tears of joy and pride—had to be tears for their Army brothers, because every Navy player knew that every Army player wanted to win as fiercely as they did.

But this year, it was all Navy, and leading the charge was Reggie Campbell. Although Navy's 294 total offensive yards weren't particularly impressive, Reggie's 227 all-purpose yards certainly were. And included in that total was a ninety-eight yard kickoff return for a touchdown—the longest in Navy history—which also made Reggie the first player in Navy history to return two kickoffs for touchdowns in a single season.

By the end of the day, Navy had accumulated its highest-ever season point total (479), and become the first of the two teams to ever beat the other team six times straight.

On the defensive side of the ball, Navy held Army to just 217 yards on offense. It was Navy's best all-around defensive effort of the year, as they tallied one sack and seven tackles for a loss, forced two fumbles, blocked a punt and broke up five passes, keeping Army scoreless in the second half.

After the game, as the teams congregated to sing, "Navy Blue and Gold," suddenly there was Reggie, standing on a ladder, conducting the Drum & Bugle Corps. Well, actually, he was trying to. He later admitted he didn't really know what he was doing. Uh, yeah, Reggie...we noticed.

Let's just hope Reggie can fly a plane better than he conducts a band.

Final Score: Navy 38 – Army 3
It was Navy's sixth straight win over Army, and their fifth consecutive Commander in Chief's Trophy.

POSTSEASON:
Poinsettia Bowl, San Diego
Navy vs University of Utah

✦

Senior linebacker Matt Wimsatt

Within a couple days of Navy's win over Army and their clinching of the Commander in Chief's Trophy for another year, Coach Johnson called a team meeting and announced to them that he was leaving Navy, and taking the Head Coaching job at Georgia Tech. I was not at the meeting, but talked to a few of the players shortly afterwards. "He'll stay for the bowl game, right?" I asked. Nope, came the response. He's gone. As of now.

My first response was a predictable mix of shock, and disappointment, and then anger, particularly when I learned he would not be taking the team to the Poinsettia Bowl.

The response of the players, however—particularly the seniors—was remarkably mature, and they helped me to keep things in perspective. There had been speculation over the past couple years that, with all of Navy's success, Coach Johnson was working his way into the national spotlight, and that he was becoming a more attractive target for larger football programs than Navy looking for a new head coach. In a sense, the players knew it was inevitable that he would leave, and probably sooner than later.

Coach Johnson had done everything Navy had asked of him. After going three-and-thirty from 2000-03, Navy had accumulated a record of forty-three-and-twenty in five years under Coach Johnson. Nobody in their right mind could have realistically predicted what Navy would accomplish in that time frame:

- *An NCAA-record three consecutive years leading the nation in rushing yardage.*
- *A record sixth consecutive win over Army—a first in the 108 year history of the rivalry.*
- *Eleven consecutive wins over the other service academy teams—one short of the all time record of twelve compiled by Air Force from 1997-2002—and five straight Commander in Chief's Trophies. (At the Navy team's Rose Garden visit with the President—a tradition for the team that wins that year's Commander in Chief's Trophy—President Bush pointed out that Coach Johnson had become a regular guest at the White House.)*
- *Five consecutive postseason bowl game appearances, a school record.*
- *A football team graduation rate of ninety-five percent, compared to the national average of sixty-seven percent.*

Being the intense competitor that he is, Coach Johnson had set his sights on the ultimate goal for a college football coach: a BCS national championship. Unfortunately, it's unlikely that that goal will ever again be within reach for Navy (although I'd love for somebody to prove me wrong!), and Georgia Tech offered, in Coach Johnson's estimation, the opportunity to pursue that goal.

The question, of course, that very quickly dominated any conversation about Coach Johnson's departure centered on who would replace him. Athletic Director Chet Gladchuck didn't waste any time in answering that question, and appointed Navy Offensive Coordinator Ken Niumatalolo—not on a temporary basis, but as the new Navy head coach.

In my view, he could not have made a better choice.

Not only was Coach Niumat the logical successor as dean of the triple option offense, and not only is he as fierce a competitor as Coach Johnson, but he truly understands and appreciates what Navy is all about, on and off the field. Like Coach Johnson, he's pretty quiet most of the time, so when he raises his voice it gets everybody's attention! The players respect him, and want to do well for him. As a man of deep personal faith, personal integrity, professional competence, genuine caring for his players, coaches and their families, and an appreciation for what Navy football is all about, I believe Coach Niumatalolo will extend Navy's winning tradition well into the future.

On a more personal level, I'm just glad I got to speak to the team before Coach Niumat at the pre-game meal in San Diego.

Gathering the team together just prior to boarding the buses to Qualcomm Stadium, Coach Niumat, in his customary soft-spoken manner encouraged the team to simply do the same things that had gotten them there in the first place. To count on each other, to play with their hearts, and to remember who they were.

Then, he said simply, "I'd like to read some names, and I'd like each of you to stand up as I call your names:

Jonathan Alvarado—Marine Corps Ground
Adam Ballard—Marine Corps Ground
Paul Bridgers—Navy Pilot
Joey Bullen—Naval Intelligence
Reggie Campbell—Navy Pilot
Ben Gabbard—Naval Flight Officer
Troy Goss—Marine Corps Ground

Antron Harper—Surface Warfare
Matt Humiston—Marine Corps Ground
Reyn Kaupiko—Surface Warfare
Chris Kuhar-Pitters—Navy Pilot
Josh Meek—Navy Submarine (Nuclear)
Matt Oberlander—Naval Flight Officer
Jordan Reagan—Surface Warfare
Dell Robinson—Marine Corps Ground
Zerbin Singleton—Marine Corps Pilot
Irv Spencer—Surface Warfare
Greg Thrasher—Surface Warfare
Greg Veteto—Marine Corps Ground
OJ Washington—Surface Warfare
Matt Wimsatt—Marine Corps Ground
Jordan Young—Naval Flight Officer"

The room sat absolutely silent, and I seriously doubt that anybody in the room—myself and Coach Niumat included—had dry eyes. By simply reading the names of the team's graduating seniors, Coach Niumat had reminded us all what we, and what Navy Football, were all about...

Facing the Anakites.
Numbers 13-14:25

"Once more into the breach, dear friends…once more!"

That's Shakespeare, in case you didn't know. It comes from his play, "Henry V", and King Henry is rallying his troops to defend against another assault by the French.

And once more we gather in preparation for a contest, this time with the awareness that it's the last time for this group of guys, and this season.

And I have one more story to tell you…

Last week, I told you the story about how Joshua encouraged the Israelites to be strong and courageous as they prepared to enter the land that God had promised them. But I want to tell you the story that sets up that one, and that tells how Joshua was chosen to be their leader after Moses died.

Forty years earlier, the Israelites were supposed to have entered the land that God had promised them. And they were perched on the edge of that land, God having set them free from slavery in Egypt and leading them to where they were. Now, this was a good land; "flowing with milk and honey" is how it was described to them. And there were people already living there, and they sure weren't going to give up the land without a fight. Like any well-planned military operation, the Israelites needed accurate intelligence about the enemy, and so they chose twelve men to conduct a recon mission, and to bring back a report of what the army of the Israelites was up against.

So the men disappeared into enemy territory, and they came back forty days later with a report of what they saw. They reported that the land was indeed full of milk and honey, just as it had been described to them. But they also said that the people who inhabited it were very strong, and the fortifications were huge. "And," they said, "there are Anakites there."

The Anakites, and their relatives the Nephilim, were giants, fearsome warriors. They were believed to be descendants of human women and angelic beings. Goliath was descended from this half human, half divine race of people. "Compared to the Anakites," the spies reported, "we seemed like grasshoppers."

So the report came back to the Israelites that if they were to attempt to take this land, they would almost certainly fail, because they could not possibly prevail against these giants. And in response to this report, the people despaired, gave up hope of ever reaching the promised land.

Except for two people, two members of the recon team, whose names were Caleb, and Joshua.

While ten of the twelve team members came back and said there was absolutely no way they could hope of taking the land, Caleb and Joshua came to a different conclusion.

"Wait!" they cried out. "This is a good land...just like God promised us! If God is with us, then we don't need to fear anybody! *We can take these guys!*"

But because the people did not have faith enough in God to lead them to victory, God delayed their entry into this promised land for forty years, and in the end only Caleb and Joshua lived long enough to finally be among those who entered the promised land.

Did you see the sports page of the San Diego paper today? In the middle of the front page of the section, in full color and bold print, is an article that starts like this:

On paper, there appears to be a problem in store for tonight's third annual Poinsettia Bowl.

On one side of the ball is the Navy defensive line, whose average size is 6 feet 2, 260 pounds.

On the other is the Utah offensive line, whose average size is 6-4, 310.

Apparently, we seem as grasshoppers to some people compared to Utah.

Especially, maybe, [defensive end] Mike Walsh, who, at six-two and 239, will be going up against Utah's tackle who stands six-seven, and weighs in at 320. That's an advantage of five inches and eighty-one pounds. Is there any of us who knows Mike, though, who doesn't feel sorry for that *other* guy? He has no idea what he's about to find himself up against!

And that's just the thing…we have a whole team of guys like Mike Walsh! Of guys like Caleb and Joshua. Of guys who don't care what the situation looks like on paper, or what the so-called experts have to say. You are a team of guys who love a good fight…who know you have something a lot more important than size or speed or even talent.

We've spent all season talking about what that "something else" is; and in reality it's a lot of things. Attitude, courage, focus, commitment, brotherhood…these are the things that are at the heart of who we are. These are the things that drive us, and set us apart.

Over the course of the season I've tried to do several things in my time with you. I've tried to faithfully negotiate the line between being your chaplain and not trying to be a coach. I've tried to offer messages that speak to you as football players, as developing officers of Sailors and Marines, and as young men of character and integrity. And I've tried to prepare you for the challenges of life—on and off the football field—by sharing stories of those who have come before us. One story a week from the Bible—the stories that form the foundation of my faith, and the accumulated truth and wisdom of a good portion of the world for the past two-thousand years that hopefully can help encourage you in your faith, whatever it may look like. And I've also relayed some stories about more contemporary situations and people.

My greatest hope for our season this year is that one of the things that you take away from this season—in addition to a Bowl Game win!—is this: an awareness of how your experience on the football field is preparing you for your lives and vocations off the field. How will football strengthen you in your professions, in your families, in your faith? Because those are the things that *really* matter.

Back to Caleb and Joshua for a minute.

Both of them were given a challenging assignment, and an opportunity to assume a role of leadership. Both of them were ready.

Is there anybody here who doesn't believe that Coach Niumat is ready for his leadership role?

Caleb and Joshua weren't stupid. They weren't delusional, Pollyanna-ish optimists. They knew the challenges and the dangers of the task ahead. But they weren't afraid. They knew their capabilities, and they believed in their God. They knew they had what was necessary, even when the rest of their teammates weren't able to see it. It's not hard to imagine—on a different team than ours—ten players slumping into the locker room after seeing the other team during warm ups, saying, "Those guys are freaking *huge!*" And then, lastly, Zerb coming bounding through the door, bouncing around the locker room like a pinball yelling, "*We can take these guys...baby!*"

The thing is, on our team, Zerb isn't the only one. We have a team of Calebs and Joshuas. And even if there is some doubt in your mind, you've got leaders like Zerb and Irv, and Reggie and Adam, all of whom know beyond any doubt that you can take these guys. And I think you all have learned to trust and follow them.

Of the twelve spies sent out, ten of them forgot to factor God's promises into their assessment of the situation, and that story is all about God's promises. So in other words, they forgot about what was most important. Ten out of twelve people "out there" look at how the stats match up in this game, and come to the conclusion that we don't have a chance. What they fail to recognize is that we are a lot more than our size and weight and speed.

There will be times in your lives when everybody else will be saying, "it can't be done." But you'll know in the depths of your heart that it *can* be done; that *you* can do it. That's when you'll have the opportunity to show that you're a leader. That will be the attitude that you will convey to your Sailors and Marines. That's the attitude that makes the Navy/Marine Corps team the most lethal, effective fighting force the world has ever seen.

Chesty Puller is quoted as saying, "We're surrounded. That simplifies the situation." Obviously, it's one thing to believe, and another to follow up your beliefs with action. But any accomplishment begins with the belief that it can be accomplished. And that takes vision, faith, imagination. It's my belief that most failures of action begin as failures of imagination. Where your hearts go, your bodies will follow.

Once again into the breach, my friends. Once again into the fire.

Trust your training, trust your preparation.

Trust your coaches and your teammates. Trust your Sailors and Marines.

Trust yourselves and your abilities, on and off the field.

Trust in God, particularly when it comes to the things that really matter.

Once again into the fire, boys. You can take these guys.

Game Wrap:

By what criteria is one to judge the success of a season?

By the team's final record? By the final national rankings? By the individual performances of the players?

In one respect, it all boils down to Wins and Losses, and there are certainly plenty of people who would insist that, in the end, that's all that matters.

To simplify a season down to two numbers like that, however, seems to me to miss something much more important, much more thrilling and evocative about college football. Are wins important? Of course! The definition of competition is to strive to win. But if wins are the only indicator of success, does that mean that losses are indicators of failure?

How do you measure things like heart? Courage? Determination? Character?

Numbers can tell part of the story, but it is only part. And, I would argue, in the big scheme of things, not the most important part. In spite of the growing evidence that college sports is viewed by many as simply a breeding ground for prospective professional athletes, I will argue to my dying breath that college athletics is much more important than that. As a current series of NCAA advertisements stresses, the vast majority of college athletes will not play pro sports, but will take what they've learned "in the arena" and apply it in their careers and vocations. Nowhere is this truer than in the military.

While there will be the occasional service academy athlete who has the potential to play sports at the professional level, there can be no confusion in the mind of every athlete that he or she is at a service academy for a very specific purpose: to prepare to serve their country in uniform. They play sports because they love to play, to compete. But they also know (or they quickly learn) that at the service academies, even competition at the highest levels (and the academies do, in fact, regularly produce national championship-level teams in many sports) serves a larger purpose: the preparation of young men and women to be officers and leaders in our armed forces, and responsible, visionary citizens of our democracy.

If the Navy football players are any indication, our country is in good hands. And the 2007 Poinsettia Bowl game demonstrated this reality clearly and dramatically.

Once again, Kaipo and Zerb sparked an offensive effort that racked up 438 yards of total offense, including 316 on the ground. Slot back Shun White and fullback Eric Kettani, both juniors, offered a preview of next year's offensive potency, accounting for 182 of those yards between them. Although Navy led for much of the first half, they had to play catch up for most of the second half. With Utah up 35-25 and 1:27 left in the game, Navy refused to lie down, and two consecutive completions from Kaipo to Zerb closed the score to 35-32 with fifty-seven seconds left on the clock.

Joey Bullen executed a perfect on-side kick, and Zerb ripped the ball from the hands of Utah's Joe Dale to give Navy the ball at its own forty-two. Unfortunately, on the second play of that drive, slotback Reggie Campbell slipped and Kaipo's pass to him was intercepted by Utah's Dale, and the Utes ran out the clock.

Navy's defense rose to the challenge, too. Irv Spencer led the team with thirteen tackles, and junior Ross Pospicil had ten tackles and an interception. Utah was forced to punt four times, and converted on only eight of sixteen third or fourth downs.

Ultimately, it was mistakes and missed opportunities that crippled Navy's effort. The most devastating mistake for Navy, however, might have been one made by the officiating crew. Late in the fourth quarter, as Utah was driving, Navy defensive back Ketric Buffin forced a fumble deep in their own territory, and the ball bounced out of bounds, hitting the end zone pylon. Everybody—except the officials, apparently—recognized that by definition that was a touchback, and the ball should go to Navy at their twenty. But inexplicably, the officials gave the ball back to Utah. Even though the Navy defense made a huge stop on fourth and one on the one yard line, Navy started with the ball at their own one instead of the twenty, and that may have made all the difference. The Mid-American Conference officially acknowledged that the officials had blown the call, and apologized to Navy. That, of course, did not change the final score.

Did that call make the difference between winning and losing for Navy?

Maybe.

But that is, after all, college football. And indeed, that's life.

Final Score: Navy 32 – Utah 35

Epilogue:
Spring Training

✦

Head Coach Ken Niumatalolo at home in the Rose Garden.

Epilogue:
Spring Training

At 0530 on a cold and dreary March morning (there is no other kind in Annapolis), seventy-three days after their appearance in the Poinsettia Bowl and the end of the 2007 season, the Navy football team shuffled onto a cold and wet Rip Miller field to begin their first team workout of the 2008 season. "Fourth Quarters" they're called, which seems a bit strange given that they're the first team workouts of the new season; but at that hour of the morning, huddled futilely inside their sweatshirts against the steadily increasing drizzle, the guys looked, in fact, like they were heading into their fifth or sixth overtime. (And, based upon their previous season, it was as good a time as any for the 2008 team to get used to playing in overtime!)

They were all there: Irv, Reggie, Zerb, Adam, Chris, Antron...the same faces, the same names, but with two significant differences. First, the seniors weren't formed up with the rest of the team, but stood on the sidelines or wandered among the players, blowing on their hands and smiling at the fact that *they* weren't there to work out. Their days of football practice were over. I couldn't quite tell if they were there to gloat, or to lend support to their teammates...probably a little of both.

The second difference was that some of the seniors were hardly even recognizable, they had lost so much weight. Ben Gabbard and Paul Bridgers, in particular, who weighed in at 297 and 268, respectively, during the season, looked almost ridiculously skinny, which drove home for me again how hard these guys have to work to keep their weight *up* during the season. (If only the rest of us had that problem!) Ironically, now they were under pressure to *lose* the weight they had worked so hard to gain during the season, in order to comply with the Navy's weight standards.

Quickly, the joking around stopped, replaced by the all-too-familiar blast of whistles and barking of the coaches, and before too long an agonizing and torturous circuit of strength, agility, speed and coordination drills was underway. The gloating of the seniors was replaced by earnest and urgent encouragement of their teammates, and I couldn't help but think that there was serious consideration taking place in the minds of some of the underclassmen about whether or not they really wanted to put themselves through this for another year. The relief expressed by the seniors at *not* having to put themselves through the pain again was plentiful and plainly evident.

And so the cycle began again, one familiar to every serious athlete, of any sport, but which plays itself out in uniquely challenging ways at the Naval Academy, and particularly, perhaps, for the football players. The end of a season leaves precious little time for "relaxing." The coaches have dispersed across the country on recruiting trips, and the next season is just around the corner.

Several weeks later, most of the coaching and support staff and their spouses gathered together to celebrate the marriage of Defensive Coordinator Buddy Green's daughter. Not all of the people at the reception were related to the football program, but the majority of them were. And I marveled at what a "family event" it felt like.

Not only did the coaches seem to have a bond like family, but so did their wives. I'd first noticed it during the season, on those occasions when some of the coaches' wives traveled with the team to a game. It was particularly evident in San Diego for the Bowl game. These women genuinely enjoy and care for each other, and it opened my eyes to what a family the Navy football community is, at all levels.

Around the same time, a couple of articles by Ivan Maisel on ESPN.com caught my eye that reaffirmed much of what I'd been hoping to convey to the team throughout the season. I was encouraged by the fact that others recognized the nature of the commitment made by these guys, on and off the field. In the first article, Maisel interviewed a couple former Navy players who were now well established in their Navy careers. One of them was Commander Kent Van Horn, who was at the time coordinating submarine operations for the U. S. Fifth Fleet. He reflected on the lessons of toughness, preparedness, teamwork and discipline that playing football for Navy taught him, and how those lessons were critical in developing his skills as an officer and war-fighter.

The second article chronicled the trip to the Middle East of an unlikely confederacy of college football coaches: Mark Richt of Georgia, Randy Shannon of Miami, Jack Siedlecki of Yale, Tommy Tuberville of Auburn, and Notre Dame's Charlie Weis. Throughout their tour of the area, and their interactions with Sailors, Marines, Soldiers, Airmen and Coastguardsmen, the coaches were in awe of the professionalism of the people, and the spirit of teamwork that they embodied. Each of the coaches reflected that their football players would have a lot to learn from these young men and women. "If athletes on any level could see how important the team was, their perception would be affected," Charlie Weis observed. "[At Notre Dame] we put signs up in January saying, 'Leave your egos at the door. These people live that creed. If you get your team to live that creed the way these soldiers do, you'll be OK."

Maisel ended his article with the observation, "It's a safe bet that all five coaches will tell all five of their teams of the maturity and teamwork they saw among the United States military. And tell them again." [Ivan Maisel, *Lessons learned on Navy football field still paying off*, and *Troops offer inspiration, motivation for coaches*, ESPN.com, 28/29 May, 2008.]

I'm glad that the coaches got to see what I've seen throughout my military career, and I'm glad that they recognize what the 2007 Navy football team helped me recognize: we are blessed with a truly remarkable group of young men and women who have devoted themselves to the service of our country.

As I write these final words, Second Lieutenants Adam Ballard and Greg Veteto are completing Marine Corps Basic School in Quantico, Virginia. Second Lieutenant Zerb Singleton will soon follow them. Ensign Irv Spencer is serving as a deck watch officer aboard *USS Gonzales*. Ensigns Reggie Campbell and Chris Kuhar-Pittars are starting Naval Flight Training in Pensacola, Florida, while Matt Oberlander is preparing to become a Naval Flight Officer. Joey Bullen is…well, he's a Navy Intel guy, so I have no idea where he is. Probably locked in a room somewhere with no windows and lots of electronic gear. For all of them, football is now a memory. After years of hard, intense preparation, they are finally doing what they set out to do.

As for me, I'm convinced that with young men and women like these stepping up to serve as leaders of Sailors and Marines, and as citizens of character and integrity, our country is in good hands indeed.

Printed in the United States
130926LV00002B/4-111/P